AMERICAN
AFTERLIFE

KATE
SWEENEY

American
Afterlife

ENCOUNTERS IN
THE CUSTOMS
OF MOURNING

THE UNIVERSITY OF
GEORGIA PRESS
ATHENS AND
LONDON

Published by the University of Georgia Press
Athens, Georgia 30602
www.ugapress.org
© 2014 by Kate Sweeney
All rights reserved
Designed by Kaelin Chappell Broaddus
Set in 9.7/14 Bodoni Twelve ITC
by Kaelin Chappell Broaddus
Manufactured by Thomson Shore, Inc.
The paper in this book meets the guidelines for
permanence and durability of the Committee on
Production Guidelines for Book Longevity of
the Council on Library Resources.
Most University of Georgia Press titles
are available from popular e-book vendors.

Printed in the United States of America
14 15 16 17 18 c 5 4 3 2 1

Library of Congress Cataloging-in-Publication Data
Sweeney, Kate, 1978–
American afterlife : encounters in the customs of mourning /
Kate Sweeney.
pages cm
Include bibliographical references.
ISBN 978-0-8203-4600-7 (hardcover : alk. paper)
ISBN 0-8203-4600-4 (hardcover : alk. paper)
1. Funeral rites and ceremonies–Unites States.
2. Mourning customs–United States.
3. Undertakers and undertaking–United States.
4. United States–Social life and customs. I. Title.
GT3203.S94   2014
393–dc23
2013016629

British Library Cataloging-in-Publication Data available

FOR

Dennis AND

Martha Sweeney,

FOR ENCOURAGEMENT

PAR EXCELLENCE

Give sorrow words; the grief that does not speak

Whispers the o'erfraught heart, and bids it break.

—SHAKESPEARE,
Macbeth, Act IV, Scene 3

CONTENTS

~ℓℓ~

~ℓℓ~

~ℓℓ~

CHAPTER 7

With the Fishes 151

~ *ele* ~

DISMAL TRADE

Anne Gordon,
Funeral Chaplain
Funerals Are Fun
175

CHAPTER 8

Death by the Roadside 183

PREFACE

I wrote early drafts of this book over three years while living in Wilmington, North Carolina, and Atlanta, Georgia. Most of the scenes—such as visits to Charleston, South Carolina, to take part in the Eternal Reefs memorial weekend and to Springfield, Illinois, to visit the Museum of Funeral Customs—took place between 2007 and 2008. I have since contacted everyone I could whose stories appear here in order to see if anything critical has changed that would alter these narratives. In one case—the story of the obituary—a great deal has changed. As it turns out, the newspaper's sharp decline in recent years adds new poignancy and perspective to the events surrounding the last Great Obituarist Conference. While most of the scenes in these pages took place in 2007 and 2008, I have also updated all information regarding trends, facts, and figures. What you hold in your hands is a contemporary tale.

Secondly, these are stories of ordinary people who find themselves involved in death and memorialization. For many, these decisions are inextricably linked to religious faith. Religion influences, to varying degrees, how people treat the dying just before and after death, when and whether they bury or cremate or both, and what these rites mean to people in the larger cosmological sense. While this work acknowledges religious beliefs, except in certain key historic moments in which they were inextricably tied to death customs, it focuses instead on personal choice as influenced by forces other than the spiritual.

Finally, it is a great responsibility to write nonfiction about people and facts outside one's personal life experiences. It's one I have taken quite seriously. I am keenly aware that I'm no historian, but rather a writer of popular nonfiction. However, I worked hard to make sure that the facts portrayed here, including historic elements, are accurate. In the years I worked on this project, I learned a little about a great many subject areas—making me marvelous at dinner parties but hardly a comprehensive master of any one of these topics. Similarly, I logged many hours of interviews and follow-up conversations with the individuals whose voices appear here. While I work in service of the story and not the whim of its subjects, I sincerely hope that the resulting work resonates as accurate in fact and in tenor. I think every good writer wishes that.

AMERICAN
AFTERLIFE

CHAPTER ONE

American Ways of Death

Jon Austin had been working as founding curator at the Museum of Funeral Customs for about a year when he had a curious visitor. His office door is always open to the lobby, so he could observe her as she neared the exit. "Thanks for visiting!" he called.

She was an elderly woman, probably in her late seventies or early eighties, and she nodded in his direction as she passed the antique carriage hearse on her way out. But then she stopped and stood completely still for a moment before turning around and returning to his office doorway.

"You didn't tell all of the story," she said.

When recounting this, Jon Austin re-creates his own confused expression: He wanted to be polite, but at the same time, he had worked hard for months to get the museum's collection of American death memorabilia just right, and so, "there's kind of this bravado in me," he says. He asked her, "What exactly have we failed to include?"

Graveyard quilt,
Nina Mitchell Collection, 1959.13, 1843.

She paused and then said, "You haven't explained what they do with the rest of the body."

And Jon Austin thought *Rest . . . ?* But what he said was, "I'm sorry. But I can't understand your question. Can you help me? Give me more information?"

She repeated it. "You haven't explained what they do with the rest of the body."

After one more confused exchange, she told him what she meant. When she was a child, a grown-up had told her that what you see in the casket is all that's present. "That's why they only open the upper end of the casket. Because that's all that's there." And now, this octogenarian asked, "What do they do with the rest of the body?"

Jon Austin's chief joy in life sprang from putting together picture-perfect exhibits like those here: the 1930s embalming room display with its gleaming metal table, the early twentieth-century home-funeral display with its chrome-plated art deco casket jacks and dark velvet curtains. These opportunities to delve into and re-create history had driven him to pursue a career as a museum director and curator. He had not anticipated ever being faced with counseling a stranger about her personal experiences with funerals and death.

He stumbled and stammered out an explanation, offering to put her in contact with a number of funeral directors, friends of his who would support his assertion that human bodies are not cut in half before being buried.

She nodded and thanked him but refused his offer. Then there was a long pause, and he didn't know what to do. "I mean, human emotion says, 'Okay. This woman needs comfort.' But how do you offer that to a total stranger in an environment like this?" In the end, he offered her some water. After she left, he collapsed into his office chair and couldn't concentrate for the rest of the day.

In his job, Jon Austin fields plenty of basic questions about the practices standard to the funeral world. Embalming. How is it done? What chemicals are used? How long does it take? How effective is it? It makes sense. No one knows about the details of embalming except embalmers. The day the elderly woman came in, however, was the first time he had to offer someone intimate guidance about her own life experiences. It wouldn't be the last. He had known this on some level from the beginning but relearns it every day: To Americans, death is an enigma.

Take the cooling board. Before my own visit to the Museum of Funeral Customs, I had heard bluesmen like Blind Willie McTell sing about cooling boards in songs like "Death Letter" and "Cooling Board Blues," but I had never seen one myself and had never attached an image to the words. Here's one: Imagine an ironing board without legs. The wooden surface of the cooling board is perforated with holes; these might be evenly spaced or might cleverly spell out the name of the manufacturer. Many were covered with cane latticework instead of solid wood. Ice was placed beneath to slow decomposition, hence the name: cooling board. When embalming came onto the scene, blood and other fluids not sucked up by embalming tubes could drain through the holes or lattice into the tray beneath.

One hundred to one hundred fifty years ago, the cooling board was the central, commonplace object involved in preparing dead bodies for funerals, a piece of furniture that predated the metal embalming tables that star in so many of today's crime investigation shows. Basically a portable platform on which to lay out dead bodies, the cooling board was a familiar if less-than-pleasant essential to everyone who lived and breathed in the decades before the advent of funeral homes. The family or undertaker used it to prepare the body, and it could also stand in for viewings when the casket did not arrive from the local carpenter or big-city manufacturer in time.

And yet a 2008 Internet image search on the term turned up nothing.

Not a single photograph of a cooling board emerged on five pages of Google. On Wikipedia, that everyman's fount of collective knowledge, the given definition left a lot to be desired. No dates—just a garbled statement about wrapping a body in a shroud in the winter and storing it in a barn until the ground thawed, and an acknowledgment of the term's popularity in a number of old blues songs. "This entry is an orphan," read a disclaimer at the top of the page. A few years later, in 2012, I did another search; this one turned up a bit more, most of it photographs. On one site, an anonymous young girl lies on her cooling board; another site features Lizzie Borden's bloodied father on his. Graphic representations far outnumber real explanatory records, though. That poor Wikipedia entry is still orphaned.

This once workaday piece of furniture has become obscure and unknown, living on only in the minds of those in funeral service and in the music of Son House. A vital rite reduced to a tinny old song on late-night radio. The tune is familiar to our bones, but heck if we can recall the words.

I didn't just wake up one morning and decide on a whim to start finding out all I could about cooling boards, cremation, and Victorian mourning jewelry made from human hair. My curiosity in these things developed because I'd been collecting stories from contemporary people involved with memorializing the dead—those who proffered various memorial choices, and those forced to make them. I was curious about the personal life story of the contemporary memorial photographer, the small-town funeral director, and the woman who had spent years tending a roadside memorial she'd created for her daughter.

But commonalities kept popping up. It turns out that the friends who remember their dead biker buddy by getting his image inked into their arms give extremely similar rationales for their choice as the family who has its patriarch embalmed, funeralized, and buried in what has become (only in the past hundred years, mind you) this country's traditional style. Purveyors of all-natural "green" burial give heartfelt arguments for what they do that sound extremely similar in some ways to a group they're often pitted against: traditional funeral directors. Meanwhile, today's explosion of options for jewelry that contains funeral ashes has a lot in common with mourning jewelry worn by Victorians.

Every time I spoke with someone about why she or he chose burial in a historic cemetery, ash scattering in the Passaic River, memorializing with a postmortem photograph, or immortalizing through ink on skin that would last forever–or at least till the bearer was gone–I heard echoes of some other answer given by someone who lived on the other side of the country or the other side of the century.

And every seemingly quirky path eventually wound its way back to the here and now–which made it all feel far less quirky. This journey, for me, was a visit to the Museum of Funeral Customs writ large. You go because it seems odd and fascinating. Sometimes it's ha-ha funny, á la the hilarity that ensues when the preacher, the priest, and the rabbi meet St. Peter at the pearly gates. What I found, though, is that on the heels of every eccentric moment emerged some poignancy: The outlandish advertising claims made of early embalming fluids ("You can make mummies with it!") and the staggering multitude of Civil War deaths that galvanized this uniquely American competition. The talk that springs up at a green-burial cemetery among a group of ordinarily taciturn men as they work to dig their brother's grave. The memorial weenie roast the family holds in his honor every year thereafter. And something always sprung up to remind me that this strange land of mourning, of memorialization, and of death itself is one for which we're all eventually bound.

Two and a half million Americans died last year. That makes 2.5 million human stories about the final decisions made for a beloved grandfather, a coworker's sister, or that guy who played guitar for spare change outside the coffee shop. I began this journey fascinated by vaults that curb decomposition for decades, urns shaped like Great Danes, and rocket-ship victory laps for cremated ashes. By the time I finished, I was wondering what these choices said about us, and about the entire American landscape of mourning.

WHAT YOU HOLD in your hands presumes to be no exhaustive history of funeral practices in America. It's a scattershot thing, this history. Like each of our stories when we lose a family member or a close friend—and this is every single one of us, sooner or later—the facts of death's history and current experience in America are strewn haphazardly across our nation's wide landscape, disorganized and largely unheard. You can find it in the memories and stories of families who work in funeral service—although many of them are reluctant to talk with outsiders, threatened as they are by drastic threats to their livelihood in the changing ways we do death. You can find it in the ancient, curling pages of nineteenth-century funeral-trade publications with names like *The Casket* and *Sunnyside*. Death's Present and Past are here and they're real, but they remain, to most of us, an unseen layer in the atmosphere of our day-to-day lives. A mystery. To most of us, what we actually know of death is only our own reaction when it touches us.

Nor does this book speculate on or predict future patterns of American memorialization. I'll leave that to the scholarly types. I'm much more interested in learning what it's like to bury your family pet at sea or to conduct five funeral services in one week or to write an obituary for a stranger. What drove Victorian women to wear black veils and scratchy black mourning crape for a full year? What was that *like*? Are there present-day American equivalents? Most of all, what of these personal stories? What made Elizabeth Stuckman choose burial in a nature preserve for her brother? Why did B. J. Dargo create an artificial coral reef from her son's ashes? Why does Mary Wilsey still maintain that roadside memorial at the spot where her daughter's car crashed?

These stories about mourning's interior worlds build something bigger. Together their echoes resound, a small note in one place playing up another elsewhere on the map or elsewhere in time. We catch glimpses of something bigger—the biggest "something bigger" we can conceive of. A death landscape that's as deep as it is wide—moreover, the landscape of our lives themselves.

Gone, but Not Forgotten

Let's start in Illinois.

Despite the extravagant unwholesomeness of its contents–the glossy embalming trocars and the jet black horse-and-buggy hearse– the Museum of Funeral Customs is, in outward appearance, wholly unassuming. One approaches more than half expecting outright kitsch. One is primed for it, in fact, by the presence, one block away, of a tourist trap shaped like a log cabin. We are, after all, in Springfield, Illinois, where it seems every other downtown building is somehow Lincoln-themed or -decorated. The log cabin across the street from the museum hawks purple plastic Lincoln backscratchers, befeathered and beglittered dream catchers of varying size and hideosity, and pennies embossed with the twinned faces of Honest Abe and John F. Kennedy sold with one of those lists enumerating twenty-two strange coincidences between their deaths.

Within sight and walking distance, the Museum of Funeral Cus-

Locket with chain of braided hair,
between 1861 and 1865.

toms seems to shrink almost visibly away from the Lincoln Log Mart (name changed because the real one is much more boring). While the latter marches right up to the road sporting a large, hanging sign announcing itself, the museum retreats behind a small square of tasteful lawn, its light pink imitation sandstone causing it to resemble a modern funeral home.

When I ask Jon Austin about the neighboring tourist shop, his polite facial expression takes on a strain, like a canvas stretched a hair too tight. "Yes," he allows, "they have some . . . interesting items for sale there." The curator of the museum is polite but firmly distancing. There's an impulse to make absurdity of his establishment too, to make death ludicrous; it's an impulse he politely denies.

Once the director of the Illinois State Historical Society, Jon has curated and directed the Museum of Funeral Customs since helping the Illinois Funeral Directors Association shape the place's design and goals eight years ago. A physically slight and conversationally intense man, he enjoys discussing the very kookiest details of American funereal history without ever quite losing the gravitas common to both funeral directors, with whom he spends a good deal of his time, and professional historians, which he is. You get the feeling he'd never use the word "kooky."

It turns out I wasn't imagining it: Jon tells me the museum's facade is indeed designed to resemble that of a modern funeral home, its salmon-colored stucco inlaid with filled-in arched window shapes just like the chapel it never was–although it sits across the street from a real funeral home and catty-corner to the hilly, manicured 365 acres of Oak Ridge Cemetery. Oak Ridge is both the final resting place of Abe Lincoln and a working cemetery with hundreds of active and available plots.

The museum is small. It takes most people about forty-five minutes to walk through its display room, Jon tells me after I finish my own walk through the place. It takes me three hours.

I can't help it. Just for starters, there are burial boxes galore here, including a small, gabled, wooden coffin that I see and immediately think, "Tiny Dracula." Tiny Dracula widens at the shoulders and comes to a point at the head, just like vampire coffins in old movies. It is meant for no monster, of course, but a nineteenth-century child. Perpendicular to its foreboding angles sits a fluffy, pink twentieth-century counterpart. A nearby sign explains that in the United States, the term "coffin" technically refers to the older, diamond-shaped container.

The term "casket" is an American death invention from the late 1800s. It comes from a French word meaning "a box containing precious valuables." The human body as a valuable jewel. In Great Britain today, they still use the straightforward "coffin," while here in the States, where we've continued to develop and elaborate on our funeral customs far beyond anything our European cousins have done, our burial boxes are no exception. The prettier "casket" prevails.

There's a respectable amount of floor space here devoted to the era that invented the casket. The display on nineteenth-century America, however, is decidedly *not* pretty. Here on view are the lives and death practices of the same people who built the most grandiose cemeteries the Western world ever saw–places like Oakland Cemetery in Atlanta and Mount Auburn outside Boston. There's something about this part of the museum that makes the hairs on my neck and arms stand straight up. It's so *morbid*. Like many an account of the Victorian era itself, it's also claustrophobic. I'm surrounded by long black dresses and jackets standing rigid and silent like empty husks. It's all *Addams Family* and photos of prairie women and their families sitting stiff, still, unsmiling.

("Victorian era" technically refers to the years 1837-1901 in Great Britain–the years when Queen Victoria reigned. Of course, the States had its own complex patchwork of historic eras during the same period. When I say "Victorian," I'm actually referring to the larger sense of the word, which encompasses domestic practices and style in the Western world during the same period.)

The Ghost of Funerals Past feels exceptionally potent in this part of the museum, and not just because of these objects' origins in Dickensian days. These items are strange in all their heavy-handed austerity, but they're also familiar. The drab clothing, hearses, and funeral processions that reached their apogee in the late 1800s pretty much cast the die for our current death traditions. Even if your own choices—say, to wear bright colors and scatter someone's ashes barefoot on a beach—stand out in stark contrast to the Victorians, your decisions feel fresh precisely because of that contrast. We're rebelling. Even now, more than a century later. Because say the word "funeral," and likely as not, in the very back of your mind, in the place where the word "funeral" finds its meaning, these old shadows still stalk.

> *The saddest of all ceremonies is that attendant upon the death of relatives and friends, and it becomes us to show, in every possible way, the utmost consideration for the feelings of the bereaved, and the deepest respect for the melancholy occasion.*
>
> JOHN H. YOUNG, *Our Deportment*, 1881,
> first sentence of chapter 26, "Funerals"

In the nineteenth century, just getting through one's day posed a higher risk than it does now. Farm work, factory work, and childbirth all held their peril. But the stealthiest killer, which made it a feat even to survive childhood, was disease. It wasn't until the late 1800s that germ theory was codified; people commonly believed that the sundry maladies that stalked them traveled in the air. In 1890, four out of five white infants lived a year. Only two out of three of all nonwhite infants lived that long. Parents, of course, were keenly aware of this; many didn't even name their children until a first birthday. By 1900, things had improved: just sixteen out of every one hundred children died before reaching a second birthday, and the average person died around age forty-seven. (By comparison, the average child born in the United States today can expect to live to seventy-eight.)

Death by whooping cough, by gangrene, and by common cold had, of course, taken place everywhere for centuries. So why did this period see a wild eruption of mourning veils, lavish cemeteries, and death poetry? It had to do with a series of sweeping changes in the ways Americans thought about the very meaning of death—and about life itself.

Strangely enough, the sumptuous cavalcade of gloom that was Victorian mourning has, as its provenance, the bright and airy Enlightenment. Without the pronounced influence of the Age of Reason in the late 1700s, none of the deathbed scenes and gloomy cortèges would have followed. For one thing, the Age of Reason recast individuals as important enough to be grieved in a major way. American colonists who had come before had been heavily influenced by the Puritan religious worldview that held humanity to be a pack of lowly, helpless wretches, bound by original sin on one side and predestination on the other. This meant that before they were even born, God had decided whether they were bound for heaven or hell, and their actions in life could never change that fate.

However, as Enlightenment philosophy trickled across the Atlantic in the eighteenth century, outlooks began to change. Thinkers like Immanuel Kant, Montesquieu, and Adam Ferguson held that the universe was governed by rational law, meaning that humans could both understand the world through reason and improve it. This bright spirit helped foster the Declaration of Independence and ideas like liberty, democracy, and the separation of church and state. And at the time, these were radical new ideas. Mind-blowing stuff.

As they caught fire, these notions spurred on an abundance of religious and philosophical ideas that themselves metamorphosed, combined, and split off as they spread from east to west through the new nation. But the two biggest ideas that most influenced death culture as we know it are evangelism and romanticism.

Evangelism began with informal services by circuit-riding ministers in places like Ohio, Kentucky, and Tennessee, and it snowballed into revival after outdoor revival. These might last for days, drawing hundreds or even thousands of families from miles around to hear the "good news" that anyone could–and should–be saved. This was a different message from the old Predestination days. The notion of human agency had trickled down from Enlightenment thinking, and if you wanted heaven, you just had to ask for it.

At the revivals, ministers from different denominations would preach fiery, emotional sermons, and the crowds would respond with similar high emotion. Sometimes people broke into frenzied dances or spoke in tongues. As one source put it, "[b]urly men sobbed uncontrollably, women barked like dogs, [and] children rolled violently on the ground."[1]

The Second Great Awakening, as the movement came to be known, was more than a series of flamboyant gatherings in the fields. It was a complete makeover of Christianity that, for the first time, depicted Jesus as a friend. This, in part, was what was so exciting about it. The movement was so popular that even people who weren't evangelical were influenced by this warm version of God and homey version of heaven–now emphasized as a place of reunion among family. This version of heaven is so familiar today that we might not even realize that it was ever seen any differently–which just shows how ingrained the evangelical model has become.

A sentimental view of God and heaven arrived at a time when other aspects of life were getting similar treatment. It was the romantic era, an age whose idealized version of hearth and home "include[ed] family prayers, reading aloud around the fireside, religious instruction of the children, and the moral earnestness of the more pious homes."[2]

Romanticism transformed the way people thought about family, life and death itself, big questions of "the ultimate truth of spiritual nature."[3] If evangelism was the common people's faith, then romanticism was the corresponding philosophy, in which anyone could find the ultimate truth through visceral experience of the natural world. Naturally, the two worked hand in glove. Both romanticism and evangelism centered on experiencing the world at its physical, emotional and spiritual fullest, to discover capital-T Truths–whether this meant wandering the forest writing poetry (romanticism) or experiencing spiritual raptures at frontier revivals (evangelism).

The ultimate romantic and evangelical experience, though, was one that would be faced by frontier people and city dwellers, Jews and Christians, poets and farmers, adults and children alike. And it was the one thing that so moved this age of romantics that they created a complex culture around it that has influenced every generation that followed.

Death marked the supreme place of mystery, the ultimate threshold between the physical world and the sublime. Poets of the era were fascinated with it. Gothic romantic writers like Edgar Allen Poe were obsessed. Death was even what motivated transcendentalist Henry David Thoreau to hightail it to the woods to "live deliberately." After his brother died of lockjaw, he went to Walden "to live deep and suck out all the marrow of life," and not "when I had come to die Discover that I had not lived."

It was this era that invented the deathbed scene. We have our dourly dressed forebears to thank for *Camille*, *Little Women*, *A Farewell to Arms*, *The Good Earth*, *Love Story*, *Terms of Endearment*, and really, every sappy movie death ever. In the romantic Victorian death, a person would die at home surrounded by loved ones who looked on as he spoke his final words–which, ideally, indicated a reunion with Christ. The idealized "Beautiful Death" was reproduced in plays, works of art, and best-selling novels like *Uncle Tom's Cabin*:

> Eva lay back on her pillows; her hair hanging loosely about her face, her crimson cheeks contrasting painfully with the intense whiteness of her complexion and the thin contour of her limbs and features, and her large, soul-like eyes fixed earnestly on every one . . .
>
> "I sent for you all, my dear friends," said Eva, "because I love you. I love you all; and I have something to say to you, which I want

you always to remember . . . I am going to leave you. In a few more weeks, you will see me no more . . . I want to speak to you about your souls."[4]

The harsh reality of dying was never quite so beautiful for most everyday people. They strove for the simpler Christian ideal of the "Good Death" in which the sufferer did not die alone and away from home or, worst of all, unsaved.

The belief in the importance of a Good Death added considerably to the emotional devastation wrought by the Civil War. As if it weren't bad enough to lose half of one's family and, depending on where one resided, possibly a great deal more, much of the heartbreak of the war lay in its destruction of the Good Death, a vital cultural convention. As historian Drew Gilpin Faust puts it, "soldiers wrote home about comrades' deaths in letters that resisted and reframed war's carnage."[5] With words on paper, they transformed terrible deaths into Good Deaths, or maybe Okay Deaths—making them a little more tolerable for their survivors.

The shocking aggregate of death brought on by the Civil War here in the States coincided with a big death culture in Great Britain, where Queen Victoria had bowed out of social life in 1861 following the death of her husband, Prince Albert. Until her own demise in 1901, Victoria absented herself from the public eye, instead hanging around her various houses clad in black mourning dress. Whether the wealthiest, chicest Brits were mostly inspired or mostly disgusted by this drastic display is up for debate. What is known is that all her life, Victoria had been a trendsetter, and that in nineteenth-century America and England alike, grief ruled fashion and custom with a grip so firm that its grasp remains at once an odd yet familiar sensation today.

The mourning for a father or mother is worn for one year. The first six months the proper dress is of solid black woolen goods trimmed with crape, black crape bonnet with black crape facings and black strings, black crape veil, collar and cuffs of black crape. Three months, black

silk with crape trimming, white or black lace collar and cuffs, veil
of tulle and white bonnet facings; and the last three months in gray,
purple and violet. Mourning worn for a child is the same as that for
a parent.

WALTER R. HOUGHTON, "Funerals,"
American Etiquette and Rules of Politeness, 1882

During the nineteenth century's golden age of death, good taste stipulated the donning of specific mourning clothing, especially for the middle and upper classes. A number of retailers made a tidy living from selling "widows' weeds," and many women of poorer classes made do by dyeing their everyday dresses and then bleaching them back again once their mourning was through.

A truly stunning guide to dress for every stage of mourning can be found in an 1881 handbook to manners by John H. Young bearing the impressive title *Our Deportment: or the Manners, Conduct and Dress of the Most Refined Society; Including Forms for Letters, Invitations, Etc., Etc. Also, Valuable Suggestions on Home Culture and Training.*

Since public grief was mainly the woman's province, it was toward her that rules of mourning were directed. Like most social arbiters of the era, Young, who took his rules from "an authority competent to speak on these matters," prescribed widows two years of mourning. During the first year–or "deep" mourning phase–they were to wear "solid black woolen goods, collar and cuffs of folded untrimmed crape, a simple crape bonnet, and a long, thick, black crape veil." Mourning bonnets ranged in style from fitted caps to huge, cone-shaped shells, and the attached veils usually extended down to a woman's waist. This first year, the widow donned little to none of the jewelry or other trimmings so dear to her era. In year two, restrictions were diminished: she was now allowed mourning jewelry, black silk, and "a shorter veil." Young's guide called for twelve months' mourning for one's deceased child or parent, six months for a grandparent or sibling, six months for "a friend who leaves you an inheritance," and three months for an uncle, aunt, nephew, or niece.[6]

To announce that they were in mourning, women trimmed their dresses with a fabric called crape, a stiff, black gauze used only in this ubiquitous corner of the fashion world. The world's chief manufacturer of mourning crape was a British company called Courtaulds, and Courtaulds made its fortune from the fabric.

There's an official history of the company penned by late economic historian Donald Cuthbert Coleman that reads surprisingly like a sly, clever gossip column. The book details the exploits both of the company's founder, George Courtauld, whom Coleman gleefully characterizes as a sort of an obstreperous boob, and of his son, Samuel Courtauld, who lofted the company to its nineteenth-century zenith of crape maker to the world.

It is a challenge to stand in the Museum of Funeral Customs, to gaze upon this now-graying trim, and to imagine fortunes being made on it. It is so ugly. Though its base material is silk, I cannot survey the dresses in these cases and even *think* that sleek, luxuriant word. The mourning crape is dull and—you can just tell—stiff and scratchy, too. It does nothing but make a dreary dress even more unpleasant. This is kind of wonderfully obstinate in the face of fashion. *Grief sucks, and while I'm experiencing it, I don't want to look pretty.*

In the great race for unpretty, companies that made crape competed with one another to an extreme. In the Courtaulds' biography, Coleman writes of "secret rooms, specially locked doors, industrial espionage, the painstaking interrogations of employees newly secured from competitors, secrecy clauses in contracts: all these and more were practiced in the course of the nineteenth century by Samuel Courtauld & Co., and some, probably all, by the small number of their competitors in the mourning crape trade."[7] At the heart of this intrigue lay top-secret methods of taking crape's raw material, silk, and dulling, crimping, and stiffening it to the consumer's satisfaction. Not some baser material, mind you. Silk. It's as if the manufacturers were working out their own grieving by bastardizing pure, beautiful things.

SHOWY DRESS

Black predominates over all colors. The showy costumes once worn
have given way to more sober colors.

WALTER R. HOUGHTON, "Dress,"
American Etiquette and Rules of Politeness, 1882

In the second half of the nineteenth century, when people were dying from epidemics, childbirth, and farm and factory accidents,
not to mention the deadliest conflict in American history–the Civil
War killed more than six hundred thousand soldiers and an undocu-
mented number of civilians–a single person's grieving periods for
different deaths were pretty much guaranteed to overlap. As a result,
a woman might wear mourning clothes for years and years when, say,
the death of her mother took place relatively soon after that of her
husband. It would be a world of darkness.

Here in the museum, the coats are made of black alpaca. The stock-
ings are black, and the long, black dresses are made of matte fabrics,
since according to governing social directives in the late 1800s, it was
disrespectful for a lady to wear anything–a skirt, pin, or button–that
reflected light during her initial period of "deep mourning."[8] She
was even cautioned against wearing undergarments that were not
black, for what if she should have to lift her skirts a bit while engaging
in some taxing activity–like, say, walking? In the nineteenth century,
semaphore and symbolism ruled over all, especially for the classes
who could afford it, and an accidental flash of white petticoats could
send entirely the wrong signal regarding a woman's true level of respect for her husband's parents who had died six months before.

The very rich could also afford to hold credence in the popular superstition that it was bad luck to hang on to old mourning clothing
following a particular grieving period. The Courtaulds' bio rushes
to point out that there is no evidence anywhere that clothiers had a
role in generating such beliefs. "They did not need to invent them,"
writes Coleman; obsessive Victorian sentimentality about death
did the job on its own, thank you.[9] Still, the practice of tossing old

mourning clothes to buy new ones certainly didn't do any damage to the pocketbooks of company executives.

The curse of the American home today is useless bric-a-brac. . . . In our chambers, perhaps, we commit the grossest violations of good taste and good health . . . a Franklin stove that is never lighted; we hang a wreath of wax flowers in a glass case on the walls, adding, perhaps, a coffin-plate to add a cheerful tone to the room; a carpet riotous with the most gorgeous roses is put on the floor, and then, after we have carefully pulled down every shade in the room, so as to exclude God's pure sunshine and get a nice, musty and cemeterial smell in the room, we have what we call, in America, a parlor.

EDWARD BOK, "Is It Worth While?"
Ladies' Home Journal, November 1900

The Victorians invented neither the knickknack nor the accessory, but they certainly engendered the hare-like proliferation of both. To be fair, the colonial Americans who had come before wore mourning jewelry too, in the form of small lockets and gold pins. In the 1800s, however, ubiquitous public mourning cranked up the popular phrase "Memento Mori," or "Remember you must die," to an ear-splitting pitch. This phrase became a pulse, a drumbeat behind an eruption of death-wear. It was helped along, no doubt, by the rise of industry and a new middle class who could afford "the niceties of a funeral, family plot and monument, along with mourning clothing and memorial arts for the home."[10]

"Memorial arts for the home" meant metal coffin plates bearing the name of the deceased, which were often removed from coffins before burial and kept as mementos. It also meant needlepoint memorializing a lost relative. In the industrial age, needlepoint kits were mass-manufactured and snapped up by middle-class women and girls, who created sofa cushions and wall hangings that bore homey mottoes such as "Absent but Not Forgotten," "Gone Home," and "We Mourn Our Loss."[11]

Wearable death mementos were also extremely popular. Along

with their black coats, dresses, bonnets, and veils, women in the latter stages of mourning sported all sorts of brooches: black and big as fists, or small and gold-framed with painted scenes. They wore black beaded necklaces that featured pendants shaped like coffins, or small hand-painted portraits or photographs of the deceased. They wore bracelets made of beaded jet, a type of fossilized coal popular for use in mourning jewelry. Jet was heavy, and one fad involved donning long chains of the stuff, some of these reaching nearly to the floor in length and several pounds in weight.

But the accessories that found the most longevity and variety were those containing the hair of the deceased. Men and women had been sporting sentimental rings and brooches with snippets of hair since colonial days, but in the late 1800s, the popularity of what came to be called "hair craft" surged and exploded into a shock of varieties. This was the golden age of young people giving their mothers or sweethearts pendants or brooches containing a portrait and a few locks of hair, sometimes woven into little mats surrounding the image. These accessories became ready-made death-wear once the son or fiancé died.

It's difficult to overstate how intricate these pieces could get. At one glass display cabinet at the Museum of Funeral Customs, I puzzle over a label. "Hair watch fob," it says. The fob is flat. It's as wide as two ordinary watchbands and long as a child's swimming ribbon, capped with gold-colored clasps, but where's the hair? Then, lightning-flash quickly, I realize that I'm looking at it. The whole fob is made of more than a dozen tiny braids of hair, interlaced to create one sleek, brown chain. It's chilling to realize that I'm looking at the actual hair of the dead person. In a way, I'm experiencing the fob as it was meant to be experienced—looking at it and speculating about the person from whom the hair came, now anonymous dust in a grave.

For decades, hair craft was the sentimental height of popular fashion. One church-produced consolation book from 1852 opines, "Of all keepsakes, memorials, relics—most dearly, most devotedly, do I love a little lock of hair; and Oh! When the head it beautified has long mouldered in the dust, how spiritual seems the undying glossiness of the sad memento! Aye, a lock of hair is far better than any picture—it is a part of the beloved object herself."[12] Ladies' magazines ran regular "How-To" columns on weaving your own hair earrings, doilies, wreaths, purses, even—ready?—tiaras.

Looking at one such project, from a midcentury issue of *Godey's Lady Book*, I imagine that the upper- and emerging middle-class housewives of the day were the first to toss their craft instructions across the room. This "Make It at Home" project from 1851 features the most intricate scene imaginable, of tiny flowers and feathers pressed in glass. It looks painstaking, delicate, and *nothing* like human hair. Except it is. Each frond and stem in the suggested project is actually dozens of strands, curled, twisted, and knotted around the thinnest of wires, which are then bent and looped to look like the tiny buds and fronds. Thankfully, one paragraph of the directions reads frankly to those would-be crafters who were not creative savants: "We now come to a branch of the hair work which depends more on the artistic skill and delicacy of touch of the worker, and on practice, than on any instructions we can give."[13]

All women's tasks of the time, from washing clothes to cooking a potato, involved a degree of complexity and sweat that would make most of us today blanch. However, while strides were taking place in the name of modernity and expedience in other realms (the early part of the century saw innovations like tin cans and matches, while the latter half saw the appearance of the sewing machine, radar, and Coca-Cola), mourning was designed to be hard. You had buried your brother; you would stay up nights over a candle sweating over the thinnest pins wrapped in his hair. You would wear scratchy clothes and mourning veils for months. It would not be convenient or subtle, and you would not be comfortable.

Were the Victorians weird? And I mean "weird" in all its uncanniest, witchiest vibrations. Standing here in the era's sea of mourning darkness certainly feels foreign. Directly in front of me, over a fake fireplace, hangs a mourning wreath. More than a hundred years ago, a real person wove this from her recently deceased mother's hair; it's both so fascinating and so repellent that I can't decide whether to take a step back or a step forward. And so, for a moment, I am locked in place, sort of rocking on my feet. Is this any odder, I wonder, than keeping a vase of one's mother's ashes in the same spot? Actually, these days many of us are likely to burn the body and then sprinkle its remains over a beautiful place we'll never return to, a beloved garden or a majestic body of water. Then there's the hippest trend of the moment: keeping the ashes close by wearing them inside a locket. It's 1860s fashion redux.

Only less viscerally so. We see hair and we think: human person. We might even know the person from her hair, which is just not true of ashes. In terms of emotion, there's something much cleaner about ashes. Something less relic-like, less macabre.

Macabre. This word is uncomplimentary. It refers to things that horrify us because of their association with death. It's a word I've never pegged on any of the who-knows-how-many violent movie and TV deaths I've borne witness to. Closing an intimate relative's eyes, shutting his mouth, and digging his grave–*that's* the stuff of my real nightmares.

Americans 150 years ago did these things all the time. I'm not saying they enjoyed them, but they did sort of *revel* in them. The long, drawn-out death scene in Victorian drama was huge, a guaranteed winner because it was something viewers could relate to. They'd all seen it half a dozen times or more, if not in such maudlin form. Social historians have made much of the parallel between these lavish death scenes and modern sex scenes in books and movies; sex and death, they say, have swapped places in the American psyche. One is overt and the other is hidden, where it once was the other way around.

The way the Victorians lingered over death went a lot deeper, however, than the clothes they wore and the jet chains they lugged around. During the period when a widow was required by social directive to cover her face in a veil and trim everything she wore with scratchy crape, she was also exempted from social obligations, especially those marked by levity. The mourner wasn't invited to weddings and wasn't expected to put in appearances at other events either. In other words, no one tried to distract the mourner, man or woman, from feeling sad. Public mourning was one time when you, Victorian mid-to-upper-class bereaved, were not expected to face your normal social obligations at all, a blessed mercy in a society utterly obsessed with appearances. And if you acted a little withdrawn or rude or crazy around other people, such behavior was entirely permissible.

Then again, there's that twenty-year-old widow forced to spend nearly two years "mourning" the forty-two-year-old husband she never really cared for. The new wife expected to go into mourning for recently dead wife number one. The second wife directed, by at least one set of rules, to mourn the death of her husband's first wife's parents. The whale-boned corset of social expectation bit both ways.

All this changed, and quickly, around the start of the twentieth century as the Victorian age gave way to something less restrained. For one thing, scientific discovery was blossoming as a means of explaining humanity's place in the world. Disease epidemics were being newly fought and prevented. Advances were being made in public health, sanitation, and hygiene, prolonging life. In a very short period of time, death itself–the everyday experience of it–was dramatically curtailed.

Take this statistic: In the waning days of the nineteenth century, the infant mortality rate was more than 125 deaths per 1,000 live births. Just forty years later, that figure had dropped to fewer than 50 per 1,000. In the same timeframe, life expectancy for adults leapt from forty-seven to over sixty. As health and science transformed the world, people saw less death, and their relationship to it changed radically. Death had always been a frequent reminder of mystery that cut across all walks of life. Now, in place of that mystery, scientifically explainable life was the source of fascination. In this new milieu, a passion play surrounding the drama of a single deathbed–Little Eva, say–seemed, well, old-fashioned and more than a little morbid.

Jon Austin, the director of the Museum of Funeral Customs, tells me that Great Britain changed its official message on mourning during the First World War. Brits were hit hard by wartime casualties, and government leaders looked out their windows and saw waves of grieving citizenry, all in black dress and black mood. Seeking to amplify morale and patriotism, they began to encourage a new message: Their soldiers had died for a noble cause; to grieve too long and loudly was to disgrace it. The idea of bucking up for the sake of country caught on, both in England and in the United States, where casualties of the Great War were far fewer. In the ensuing decades, especially Stateside, people tossed their widow's weeds, and public mourning times were abridged from years to weeks.

The etiquette books changed too. Rather than emphasizing the importance of sufficient displays of grief, the new guides focused on tastefully suppressing it. A 1923 etiquette author named Lillian Eichler spends three of twenty pages on funeral decorum railing against the tastelessness of Victorian mourning accessories, processions, and pomp. She calls such emotionality "savage" and writes, "Simplicity characterizes the entire service among well-bred people everywhere."[14]

Such standard-bearers of politesse spoke, and people listened. It did not take long for the old adornments of death, once discarded, to grow cobwebby and strange. The United States in the early twentieth century was absorbed with progress and modernity, and by the late 1920s, the same craft magazines that had once printed how-to guides for hair jewelry ran articles about the concept as a strange historic curiosity. By 1945, after a second world war, a writer profiling the antique practice for *Hobbies* magazine writes, "The gruesome idea of wearing jewelry made from the hair of a loved one who had died is hard for the matter-of-fact person of today to grasp."[15]

For the practical person of 1945, mourning looked much like it does today. Remembering and grieving the dead had transformed from an official process with a sanctioned public face to an amorphous something one "got over" in private. The First World War had introduced the idea that the dead soldier was someone you shouldn't grieve "too much," and the notion of bravery in the face of grief spread to people mourning civilians in peacetime, too.[16] This shift in feeling was no natural, grassroots movement; it was prescribed. The 1923 etiquette manual penned by Eichler is filled with contempt for gauche citizens who still brought their grieving into the public eye. In a sea change from the books of forty years before, Eichler recommended that "[t]he ladies of a bereaved family should not see callers, even the most intimate friends, unless they are able to control their grief. It is a source of discomfort to the visitor." Along with other social standard-setters of her time, Eichler urged the woman whose grief was "uncontrollable to strongly consider absenting herself" from the funeral of her husband or child, not because it was unladylike to attend funerals, but to prevent disruption. "With the growing taste for privacy and simplicity," she wrote—and pay especial attention to the choice of verb—"foolish demonstrations of grief, expressed in outward display, have been eliminated." *Eliminated*. It calls to mind the caprice in a shift in hemline, or some deadlier move.

In terms of fashion, the wearing of black during this period was still accepted. However, a key difference emerged: "There is no iron-clad rule concerning mourning," writes Eichler, "and one may or may not wear it."[17] Suddenly, mourners were given the option: You could let the world know through your clothing and your behavior that you were mourning, or not. Everything else in the chapter, however, fairly screamed for its "elimination" as quickly as possible. The rebellion had begun. And in this way mourning retreated from public rite to private practice. It went underground.

Sarah Peacock,
Memorial Tattoo Artist

Under the Skin

The churchyard scene in the photograph is sepia and sprawling. Its blocky crosses and headstones, hemmed in by grasses grown long, look like they belong to a land somewhere between old New England and *Tales from the Crypt*. Some of the stones bear names, others don't, and there's still plenty of empty space where more monuments will appear later. This is no actual graveyard I'm looking at, but a tattoo, a work in progress that will eventually cover the entire broad back of Randy, a local biker. More names will appear on the stones each year as his buddies ride off to that motorcycle rally in the sky. The tattooed graveyard scene is a traditional way for bikers to honor their dead. The creator of this tableau, Sarah Peacock, is not specifically a biker tattoo artist, although she lives in the same coastal town as me–Wilmington, North Carolina–where a good number of motorcycle dudes and ladies also make their home. She does tattoos for college professors too, and real estate agents and restaurant workers.

A fair number of these clients are motivated by the loss of a child, a grandparent, or a sibling.

"Well, there's nothing more permanent than a tattoo," says Sarah when I ask her why death makes people want to ink themselves. "There's nothing more symbolic than to permanently etch your skin, in memoriam, to someone else." She is leaning over the right bicep of Eric, a middle-aged guy with a handlebar mustache. With long-taper number-twelve stainless steel needles, Sarah uses quick strokes to insert ink into the epidermis. Her wild red hair is corralled into its usual two braids, each looped upon itself, and her skin is mapped out so completely in tattoos that it appears a grayish blur when she moves to speak or change out ink. Her clear blue eyes are lined with creases; right now they are flat and intent on her work.

When she finishes and Eric leaves, his shoulder will be newly em-blazoned with three cubist horses charging toward the foreground and one doe-eyed pony. These stand for Eric's family. The pony is his baby daughter, born one month ago. He chose horses because they're strong and beautiful and also for superstitious reasons: Tattooing the names or real portraits of the living is bad luck.

There is something in Sarah Peacock's Yorkshire accent and low no-bullshit voice, even before you consider the proud way she carries herself or her own impressive cloak of tattoos–the first one inked, to her parents' horror, in 1987, in Peterborough, England, a place and time when girls definitely did not get tattoos. "I met a woman with a tattoo, the first woman in my seventeen years," she says, "and soon as I saw that tattoo, I was like, 'It is on.'" She snuck out of the house to visit the only tattoo parlor she knew of, where she got a small tribal-style butterfly on her left shoulder blade. It's a tiny, faded creature now, dwarfed and crowded over by dozens of other designs, so many she has lost track. This doesn't bother her. Her own mul-titudinous tattoo experiences blend together in her memory, and the finished product on her skin seems almost beside the point. In-stead, she exists entirely in the moment between the ink she has just laid down and the ink she's about to apply, always with a clear-eyed, placid anticipation of what's next. Before she even tells me it's her job to remain a calm and focused guiding light to clients in distress, I believe her.

Her voice has a way of sounding quiet and commanding even though everything she says to me today is spoken in a half-shout over the electric needles—her own and that of an employee a few feet away in the next room. I've come here to ask Sarah about the memorial tattoos she has created over her fourteen-year career. Before Sarah was a widely respected, award-winning tattoo artist, she was a painter, and she still is. She specializes in realistic portraiture in her tattoo work, inking sepia or brilliantly colored images of people's idols, pets, or grandparents into their backs or arms or chests. A lot of people who want memorial tattoos want portraits. End result: Sarah Peacock does a lot of memorial portraits for people. They probably account for 10 percent of her business.

When Sarah creates tattoos to memorialize the dead, it usually goes like this: Earlier this year, she inked a man whose wife had died of a fluke illness at the age of thirty-eight. Sarah worked from a photo the man had. "And he said that getting the tattoo was his last stage of letting go. So when I finished that portrait, he cried."

Or it goes like this: In the spring she did a pair of tattoos for the father and brother of a man in his early twenties who attempted to hang himself, failed, and then died in the hospital a few days later. "And when the father came in to book the appointment, he was nearly in tears," she tells me. "So I was expecting it to be a really emotional experience, but actually, when he got the tattoo, he was able to talk about it. And it was interesting, psychologically, because I think the booking of the appointment was his letting go. So actually getting that piece was a celebration."

This idea of letting go of someone by having that person permanently set into your own skin seems counterintuitive. After all, that image is there every day, forevermore. But rather than a sign of obsession, Sarah finds that a tattoo of the deceased usually demonstrates the opposite.

"You know, I think that for a person to be able to look at an image day after day after day shows that they have gotten to the point that they've let go of that control. Normally for a while, there's some avoidance there; they can't face it. But if they can look every day at that portraiture, they have gotten to the point where they're no longer avoiding it."

A few years ago, Sarah started taking yoga, and she has absorbed the practice's ideas of freeing oneself from physical and material attachments. I already referred to her as "award-winning," but my information on that is limited to the following: Sarah Peacock won Tattoo Artist of the Year at the North Carolina State Tattoo Convention in 2002. She won "Best Sleeve" at a convention in Virginia in 2004. She's always showing up in tattoo mags like the charmingly named *Prick*, and she has appeared on a Discovery Channel documentary called *The Human Canvas*. Every detail I learn, however, I don't learn from her. "I've thrown all those out," she says vaguely when I ask about her accolades.

Similarly, she almost never talks about the work itself, the inked designs she spends hours on. She talks instead about what led the person to come in and get the tattoo, and what sort of mood distinguished the experience. After every story, I have to ask her to go back and describe the end product. That's the way it is now. I ask her to describe the tattoos the father and brother got, and she shuts off her needle for a moment.

"Oh . . ." into the sudden, ear-ringing quiet. "A portrait of the son at two different ages. The brother wanted to remember his brother when he was younger, and not so . . ." She pauses. "Well, his brother went out of his *mind*," she says, with a shake of the head, "but the father wanted the portrait at the age that he was when he tried to commit suicide."

———————

Even if most of her memorial tattoo clients come to her when they're no longer gripped by the first sharp shock of grief, I can't imagine that this work wouldn't be emotionally trying.

"No," she says quickly. "It's just a part of the larger job: You have to keep calm," she says. "My role is to have that person be as comfortable as possible, and I'm not avoiding the issue of why they're getting tattooed."

But she's not just some mother figure with a septum piercing, either. Unlike the barkeep or the beautician, Sarah Peacock is not peddling numbing inebriation or a new look; she's inflicting physical agony. "The tiny kisses of kittens," she calls the needle's stabbing action, grinning for a moment. It's not just the permanence of the finished product, but the discomfort inherent in the process that draws people in mourning to translate an emotional throbbing into a physical one and emerge intact on the other side with a beautiful scar.

People whom she shepherds through this difficult stage view her as sort of a modern shaman. After several intense hours of partnership with them, she doesn't see them again. It reminds me of this: You know that friend who hangs out with you in your bad days following the divorce, whom you feel weird calling later once things are better? And whom you *don't* call? Not because you no longer like the friend, but because in your mind, he's now inextricably linked to the darkness. While she receives, and counts on, a ton of repeat business, the people Sarah sees just for memorial portraiture are people she expects to lose immediately and forever. This is true of the father and son who got the portraits. "I know I'll never see those guys again. *Hopefully* I won't see them again." It's not that she didn't like them; just the opposite. She wishes them well.

This also means that she'll never again see the piece of art she worked so hard to create. It's strange. The tattoos that grant the honored dead a sort of new existence also mean the sure passing of her work from her own world forever. She calls this "a good lesson to have learned as an artist" and compares it to spring cleaning. "If you empty your surroundings, you empty yourself in order to create more," she says. "Nothing's permanent."

She has said no to hundreds of prospective clients because the tattoos were not her style or up to her taste standards. But Sarah Peacock never refuses a tattoo to honor the dead. "No, I don't mess with memorial stuff. That's very personal to them." If you ask her to, she will tattoo a simple cross and an "RIP" symbol and be done with it. She'll ink a pair of initials, or pretty much anything else you like.

Other designs are to be avoided, however. There are superstitions about life and death in the world of ink. She tries to caution people against getting tattoos of the objects of romantic interest. She does this because of the mutability of human affection—"I mean, you're pretty much branding yourself," she says. But she also believes that tattoos of living sweethearts are bad luck. She's talked people out of getting the names of girlfriends, and even husbands and wives. "I'm like, 'Don't do it, dude,'" she says, and Eric, the guy under her needle at this moment, chuckles.

"I think it's bad juju to get a name," he says.

"It is!"

What about sons and daughters? Nieces?

Those are fine, says Sarah.

But Eric doesn't agree. He says that the same tattoo that connects you permanently with the soul of the departed can sever you in this life. He puts enough credence in the superstition to avoid any but oblique references to the living in any of his tattoos, hence today's horses on his shoulder. He has no intention of letting go of his newborn daughter just yet.

Tattooing culture in this country can be traced back to that of European sailors, whose capricious world was bedecked in superstition. It makes sense; humanity's storied view of the sea has always been that of an alluring place of unpredictable peril. Superstitions brace that world with clear-cut rules, the sense of order humans crave. On levels macro and micro, we are always looking to ascertain cause and effect. We string lines of meaning across space where none is inherent so that we can rest our heads there without fear. From territories geographic and emotional that we cannot control or predict, we make provinces for rules we cannot test, because any illusion of predictability makes us feel safe. The realm of human relationships is like the ocean. It is governed by the mercurial feelings and decisions of people who are not us—our enigmatic husbands and girlfriends—and by earthly chance we cannot control. My grandmother was a firm believer that you should hold your breath when you pass a cemetery. That pregnant women should not attend funerals. That sweeping under the bed of a sick person will cause him to die, and leaving a hat on a bed courts the Dark Angel, too. I could not argue with her on these points, and frankly, some part of me was always too chicken. One cannot decisively prove that it is not bad luck to tattoo your skin with the direct image and name of a living person; you can only point to all the bad things that have befallen those who have. Death is about as biddable as the ocean or the whims of other people.

Sarah Peacock has inked the sepia image of a four-year-old child onto a bereaved mother's back. She has inked the word "cholo" in Old English script into the chests of members of Latino gangs. She has tattooed dark teardrops inches from the eyes of young men. Tears are common prison tattoos, traditionally meaning that the bearer has killed someone. That meaning has expanded to signify mourning as well. She has tattooed the images of pet Chihuahuas and husbands, of crosses simple and ornate, of banners emblazoned with names on torsos and forearms, and of gravestones with dates.

The graveyard scene across the back of biker Randy reminds me of the family quilts that colonial women used to make. The design on the quilt was of a fenced graveyard, surrounded by coffins with family names stitched on each. The quilters moved the coffins into the quilt's center once the person died. Except quilts, unlike tattoos, can last for generations. They hang in houses and folk museums. Sarah Peacock's canvas is living and breathing; it has a finite lifespan. And it's this vitality and subsequent mortality that makes them remarkable, these death tattoos that Sarah hopes never to see again, portraits of the beloved dead, the pain of whose death the living hoped to extinguish somehow by prolonging their likenesses, flat, breathless, and still, on their own skin. Until they're gone, too.

REVEALED:

*How graveyards
became cemeteries*

CHAPTER THREE

The Cemetery's Cemetery

In southeast Atlanta, Memorial Drive and Boulevard meet at a crush of hip new lofts, tire shops with hand-painted signs, tree-shaded Victorians, and cars careening too fast down asphalt that's potholed and gritty. Walled in at the corner of these two thoroughfares lies Oakland Cemetery. It sits quietly here, has for years, at the center of a number of neighborhoods described at various times as substandard, crime ridden, revitalizing, gentrifying, exorbitant, blighted, and rejuvenated. You can see its sculpture from the street, elaborate statues and obelisks poking out above the tall brick wall that separates Oakland's extravagant decay from The World.

Like so many things launched in the Victorian and Edwardian eras–the architecture of our nation's great libraries and the Coca-Cola Santa Claus among them–burial grounds like this one have set a blueprint in the collective imagination. Oakland is everything we think of when presented, out of context, with the word "cemetery":

Lithograph, woman mourning by tomb,
D. W. Kellogg & Co., between 1840 and 1842.

wrought-iron gates and crosses poking out of grassy ground, some straight and others at jauntier angles—all the ingredients of childhood drawings at Halloween. Oakland is the cemetery's cemetery. It's a place to lose oneself in the strange beauty of a verdurous death playground built by our Victorian ancestors, a place to learn why this kind of cemetery is what we think of when we think of cemeteries and to find out why cemeteries like this aren't built anymore.

I love tours. Tours with guides and tours with books. Official tours in buses and unofficial tours with friends on bicycle. I even love self-guided tours with out-of-date museum-issued pamphlets characterized by bewildering layout and syntax. So I'm undaunted when Mary Woodlan, who coordinates the volunteers and special events at Oakland, tells me one March day in 2008 that I've missed the guided-tour season by exactly one week and will have to guide myself.

"And I'm sorry. This is really hard to follow," she says, handing me the cream-colored self-guided-tour pamphlet. "New pamphlets are actually coming out next week."

Like most people in charge of outreach at successful places that depend on the public's generosity to survive, Mary is accommodating and friendly. She agreed to an interview on very short notice, interrupting her packed-to-the-gills part-time workweek. And now she has *given* me the booklet, which costs three dollars at the gift shop, while apologizing for its shortcomings. I take it, nodding a lot and thanking her, hardly glancing at the thing as I fold it into my bag.

So the next day, I'm armed for my tour. When my friend Jon and I pull up and park, we take out the pamphlet. Its cover features an ink-jet print of the cemetery's Victorian obelisks, headstones, and mausoleums, a skyline of sorts against the backdrop of Atlanta's real skyline. It's a fuzzy picture that somehow manages to make Oakland look less impressive than it is in real life. Superimposed across it are the words "Oakland Cemetery: Atlanta's Most Tangible Link."

"Link to what? The underworld?" Jon asks when I charge him with holding the booklet. Later I learn it's actually a quote from historian Franklin Garrett, who called this place "Atlanta's most tangible link between the past and present." And it's exactly this sense that draws us here. In a city with a serious reputation for tearing down the old in favor of the new, places with any real connection to history feel especially charmed. In the case of Oakland–a rambling old park literally dedicated to the dead–the atmosphere is almost otherworldly.

Jon has come along with me because he's an old friend whose geeky interest in all things historic intersects handily with my geeky interest in old cemeteries. I also need someone to help juggle my array of gear. For aside from (1) the Most Tangible Link booklet, whose centerfold includes a map with numbered landmarks, I've also brought along (2) a second map. This one color-codes the cemetery's twelve sections and contains its own numbering system to highlight the set of graves *it* deems notable. During our walk, I will also charge Jon periodically with carrying (3) a trade paperback I bought at the cemetery gift shop, a book that forced $19.99 from my credit card through the sheer power of cool historic photos. (Possibly the coolest was snapped around 1910. It's taken from the same spot as the Tangible Link pamphlet's cover, so the photo features an earlier version of the city skyline, in which the chalk-white headstones swim in a tangle of knee-length grass, hedges, and spindly trees.) My camera (4) is slung around my neck, and finally, I have (5) a handheld audio recorder at the ready to capture the epiphanies we're bound to have along the way.

I am properly outfitted. Ready. To interpret, document, and record. As if there's a proper beginning, middle, and end to this stroll through forty-eight sprawling and only sort-of organized acres; it's just up to me to locate and tag them.

When we set foot inside the black iron gates that mark Oakland's main entrance, there's a palpable hush as the hubbub of the outside world disappears into a wash of green-gold light. We set about orienting ourselves. The canopy of tall oaks the place is named for, some of the oldest in the city, filters the sunlight percolating down through the draped Spanish moss onto a wide, black avenue with raised blocks on every side. The blocks are populated with all manner of headstones, obelisks, and statuary. The temperature seems to drop a little.

This is the cemetery's oldest section, the original six acres purchased from a farmer named Alfred Wooding in 1850. We are ready to start my neat chronological arc, beginning with the cemetery's very first burial. Jon pulls out the Most Tangible Link and I pull out the small map. We consult.

Then we start off in different directions.

Instead of neat city blocks—or something like, say, a tree farm—each square's forty by seventy feet or so is really more like an actual forest. In my search for the first grave, I trip around markers of all sizes, shapes, and materials. The stones perch all over, in relationships to one another we can hardly begin to detect. There are individual stones standing alone and others in small familial clumps, facing every direction. Most are so old that their writing has been worn down to nothing. They are flat, round, rectangular, flush with the ground, or fashioned into statues. There are small pillars and granite trees climbing with granite vines. Then again, I think, it is something like a real city: We try for organization, we live on this road or that block, but our actual lives, unkempt things, spill out all over.

We have to grant some latitude to the people who created burial places like these back in the mid-1800s. When shovel first hit dirt to lay someone to rest here, the cemetery as we know it was a concept brand new to the United States. The term was used occasionally in Europe, but in early nineteenth-century America there were only graveyards, and city graveyards were little more than places to bury bodies. No one thought of them as places you'd visit, so not much planning went into their design.

One nasty night in Paris helped change all that. In his wonderfully detailed book on cemetery development in this country, *The Last Great Necessity*, David Sloane tells of an extraordinary convergence of events that began with a centuries-old graveyard in downtown Paris called the Cimetière des Innocents. One evening in 1780, residents in an apartment building next to the cimetière "were overwhelmed by a stench rising from below, and several became seriously ill from mephitic gas." The overcrowded graveyard had "broken down the basement walls and sent over two-thousand partially decomposed bodies into basements."[1]

At this time citizens from London to Boston were complaining of overcrowded family crypts raising a stink, and of poorly buried bodies popping up here and there. These dismal episodes helped spur the movement that resulted in the founding of France's famous Père Lachais Cemetery in 1804. Père Lachais was the first of the great rural cemeteries, the funerary answer to the burgeoning romantic movement. Unlike plain old graveyards, which were like landfills for bodies, rural cemeteries were *designed* to be visited by the living. Like the popular public parks that were being established at the same time, rural cemeteries were restful, reflective places of tamed nature. Families were encouraged to stroll along the new, winding pathways, to plant greenery and place pretty monuments on their loved ones' plots.

As a cultural movement, romanticism was obsessed with nature and questions of the life/death divide. In the rural cemetery movement, this focus translated to an environment that would inspire reflection about both. Rural cemeteries were pastoral, picturesque places outside the busy city centers, where tamed natural beauty and works of art met to inspire contemplation.[2] Within three decades the trend had hopped the Atlantic, and rural cemeteries began to spring up along the east coast right when the accompanying Victorian death craze was at its height in the mid-1800s.

As in a lot of other towns, the public graveyard that Oakland replaced was located in Atlanta's center, and though no grisly cave-ins had taken place there, city leaders were concerned about the possibility of nearby residents becoming ill from corpse-tainted soil and groundwater. The city purchased a remote, pastoral property for the new cemetery primarily because of its perch high on a hill east of the city (almost a full mile!).

Still, while Oakland was pleasant compared to the dismal old grave-yard, like most rural cemeteries of the era, it was still far from neatly organized. As with most new cemeteries started around this time, his-torical records on the identities of those buried here are few, and after nearly thirty years of restoration work, Historic Oakland Foundation volunteers still come upon undiscovered old graves and pieces of an-cient monuments and statuary in their work mending and gardening. It's less museum, more archeological site.

It hasn't been ten minutes and already the cemetery is working its glamour on us. Already it has beguiled me out of my straightforward quasi-academic mission. Jon has disappeared several blocks away be-hind a thicket of taller monuments, and several more minutes go by before he calls out, "Dr. James Nissan?"

"That's it!" I click on my audio recorder and rush over. They're two slightly different realities, the locations of Oakland's first burial in the three-dimensional world and on my map.

Looking at Dr. Nissan's headstone, there's frankly not much to remark upon. Despite the ostensible glory of being number one, his grave is nothing like those of some of his neighbors whose large head-stones are engraved with Bible verses, poetry, flowers, and crosses. His headstone is both small and, at this late date, blank. The first per-son to be buried in Atlanta's oldest cemetery is no town native. In-stead, Dr. N was just passing through from parts unknown when he died of a mysterious illness. Like so many people of *his* time, he had a tremendous fear of being buried alive and asked the attending doctor to cut his jugular vein after he was pronounced dead. At least that's how the story goes, according to the modern bronze plaque sitting in front of the old headstone, its five lines the sum total record of what is known about Dr. Nissan's existence here on earth.

For all the sixty-seven entries in the walking tour and the 126 pages in my paperback, a handful of stories like this one are really all that's known about most of the people Mary Woodlan endearingly calls "our residents." A sort of motherly affection invaded her voice when she spoke of those buried here. It was sweet, as if these dead were her helpless wards.

And in a way, they *are* orphans. From the beginning, the city had no caretaker role over Oakland's plots, but instead sold them outright. People bought them and then held complete responsibility over the graves forever after, from choosing what plants or markers to place at the graves, to tending to their upkeep forever. This was in line with common practice all over the country before the late nineteenth century, when in a matter of decades, the process of death and dying was taken over by professionals and jobs like landscaper and embalmer began to distinguish themselves. There were other inventions too: The notion of uniform cemetery landscaping. The funeral home.

And perpetual care–the notion that a cemetery would be responsible for basic upkeep forever. Oakland never instituted perpetual care. While the nation's other cemeteries began to establish funds for maintenance and keep track of the histories behind the people they buried, Oakland just kept doing things the old way. Some individual families established trusts with local banks or the City of Atlanta for upkeep of their family plots, but many of those have long since run dry.

"Oakland is essentially unknowable," said Kevin Kuharic, the cemetery's landscaping and restoration director. For a long time there was a dispute over the number of Atlanta mayors buried at Oakland–was it twenty-five or twenty-six? (At the time of this printing, Oakland has placed the official number at twenty-seven. Former mayor Ivan Allen was moved here from another cemetery in 2009.) History here is pieced together year by year, by historians and archaeologists. No wonder Mary feels such ownership. These graves–of people without living descendants–are all hers.

What *is* known about Oakland is just as compelling: It's the final resting ground of five Confederate generals and six Georgia governors. Author Margaret Mitchell and golfer Bobby Jones are buried here, too. There is no special section for celebrities or politicians; they're mingled in with some seventy thousand others. Oakland has its divisions too; there is the old African American section and the former Potters' Field. Also specially demarcated are Jewish Hill, the older Jewish Flat, and the Confederate burial grounds. The cemetery's other, more diverse sections are called Knit Mill, Bell Tower Ridge, and Hogpen Corner, where Farmer Wooding's swine once lived. There's also Greenhouse Valley and Roger's Hill. No one knows why Roger's Hill is called Roger's Hill.

As we walk along the southern edge, the cemetery blocks soon grow thick with showy monuments. We negotiate obelisks, statues, and mausoleums–those one-story granite cabins for all the family–and soon we're standing at the foot of an imposing arch that looks ancient in these surroundings. The arch is seven feet high and emblazoned with the name "Kontz" in heavy block lettering, above which flies the spread-winged sun god Ra. A pair of carved lotus plants blossom on the arch's two legs. The Kontz arch looks like it belongs at the foot of the Sphinx instead of here in this green place. Egyptian Revival architecture was all the rage in the mid-1800s, when Christian Kontz was hard at work designing his family's death monument. By weird coincidence, this popularity intersected with the American rebirth of embalming, a practice first perfected by King Tut's people.

As status symbols, showy grave markers like this one were hot items in the 1800s, an era when people were spending a lot more time at cemeteries than generations who came before or after. Cemeteries grew to be popular weekend haunts for courting couples and picnicking families, just like the new public parks that were sprouting up at the time.

But for the sentimental Victorians, the new cemeteries had a special something that no regular park could match: death. Reading some Wordsworth at a park to that girl you were courting was fine– but it took on a special thrill when "'Mid crowded obelisks and urns."

All over the country, rural cemeteries had become so heavily trafficked with pedestrians that newspapers ran opinion pieces about them, such as this wry 1861 take on Mount Hope Cemetery: "Drinking saloons are being erected in the vicinity of the Cemetery and dance houses were [*sic*] expected to soon be seen there. The time will soon come when painted harlots will revel with freedom in the grounds."[3]

Of course, the newspaperman who wrote that opinion didn't know it, but the popularity of the cemetery had reached its height. And since the people who bought the plots held carte blanche in terms of their appearance, it made for a bold, anything-goes period in cemetery development. As a result, many old cemeteries like this one resemble competitive sculpture gardens, with one family's intricately carved mausoleum dwarfed by another family's angel with outstretched arms, both of these surrounded by soaring obelisks built ten or twenty years later as the industrial age steamed ahead. Christian Kontz wanted a monument that would stand out, one that would last for the ages, like the Egyptian pyramids that inspired him. If the one-hundred-plus years between Kontz's death and this moment is any measure, the man succeeded. Any time you drive by the cemetery and glance up, the Kontz arch is the first monument you'll notice, the one that stands out from the jungle of elaborate markers just inside Oakland's walls, all competing for attention still, years after the courting couples and gardening families have gone home forever to their own reward. Still, even with the noise of cars flying past on the gritty commercial strip on the other side of the wall, one can almost hear the popcorn hawker's voice on the breeze.

To say that the Kontz arch stands apart is not to say that it stands alone, not in terms of elaborate design. Beyond inventing evangelical death mottoes like "Not Dead–Only Sleeping" and "Gone Home," the Victorians also developed their own language of death symbols. For example, in this section of Oakland, tall angels grasp long torches. These translate to a life snuffed out too soon. One wouldn't place a torch-bearing angel atop the grave of an aged father who died peacefully in his sleep. Two clasped hands on a headstone mean the deceased are a set of parents. Meanwhile, the founding fathers' obelisks and columns, vying for attention with their impressive heights and girths, stand, not surprisingly, for "abiding life." Which, when looking up at one, reads rather like a euphemism for something more anatomical.

Small sculptures of cradles or lambs mark the graves of infants– except in the case of Ms. Molly Weimer's mockingbird, named Tweet. When Tweet flew on to the next life in August 1874, Ms. Weimer requested that the sculptor carve his likeness to perch on his plot. The stonecutter, however, did not know how to make birds, only lambs; so a lamb is what Tweet got.

It's comforting to look at a stone anchor leaning against a cross and know what to make of it (the deceased's hope and faith, and maybe a seafaring life). At least in this sense, my mission to decode the cemetery feels like a success. In an age when the Grim Reaper held terrifying and unpredictable sway, the ability to use graves to tell stories about one's dead mother or husband must have granted some comfort to surviving kin, too. If death saddened and destroyed, at least you could put up a monument whose evangelically influenced language would transfigure an individual life into something easily decipherable and lasting. Religious faith aside, these stones gave the deceased a life beyond death itself, just as memorial markers do today. But step back and trip on the monument behind you, lose your focus for just a moment, and the place is again rendered incomprehensible.

If Oakland looks wild now–and it does, compared to your average memorial park–it's nothing compared to how it looked in your great-great-grandmother's day. As it was the vogue for rural-style cemeteries to maintain a pastoral air, Oakland's founders allowed many of the trees and much of the shrubbery from Farmer Wooding's days to stand. Grass grew long around the monuments in Oakland's heyday, and families planted their own gardens and trees, too. It retained much of its undomesticated feel as late as the 1950s, when the city removed a number of hedges and plants to cut back on maintenance costs. By then, the cemetery had fallen into great neglect.

With the passing of years, the funeral world had become the funeral industry. Other cemeteries streamlined their landscapes and instituted special maintenance fees for the upkeep of graves and walkways and monuments. The city of Atlanta, which ran Oakland, did none of this. The nineteenth and twentieth centuries passed, and with them so did many of the original families who had purchased graves and held funerals here. They'd moved away, stopped coming, or just died out.

Even today, with nine or ten burials still taking place here each year, the old Victorian policy holds: People are responsible for their own burial plots, forever, period. While paid contractors mow the grass, pick up leaves, and empty trashcans, families are supposed to take care of everything else. In reality, most upkeep is done by the Foundation, which runs overwhelmingly on volunteer power. Restoration director Kevin Kuharic calls the issue of maintenance at Oakland "the problem that never goes away." The city still operates the cemetery at a financial loss, and now that all the grave spaces have been bought, burials will decline year by year, and conditions will continue to deteriorate. The only hope for the place is the tourists.

A lot of tourists come to see the cemetery's next section. Jon and I are heady with Victorian flamboyance, drunk on angels and flowers and finery, so when we round the next bend, I'm taken off guard. There's something of a visual stun when we reach the Confederate Memorial. Small plain markers of white march on, row upon endless row. This section was modeled after Arlington National Cemetery, and though it's smaller, the effect still astonishes: between where we stand and the next ridge, the arrangement of thirty-nine hundred evenly spaced graves lobs a sucker punch at one's perspective. (It's interesting that Oakland should mimic the style of Arlington, a cemetery whose acreage was bitterly appropriated in 1864 strictly for the burial of Union dead. It was Northern general Montgomery C. Meigs who, at the height of the war, proposed taking over the Lee family estate for the interment of Northern soldiers. "His intention," reads that cemetery's website, "was to render the house uninhabitable should the Lee family ever attempt to return.")

At the foot of the hill, the markers surround a three-story obelisk, which remained the city's tallest structure for years after it was dedicated by the Atlanta Ladies' Memorial Association in 1874. In this way, Oakland is reminiscent of another cemetery dedicated about the same time: Gettysburg, where soldiers' graves surround Soldiers National Monument, commemorating the Union victory there. Gettysburg is also known for pioneering a design in which every solder's grave is identical, regardless of rank or station–a design repeated at Arlington and also here at Oakland, to slightly dizzying effect.

The work of the Atlanta Ladies' Memorial Association, or ALMA– which raised the funds to put up the Confederate obelisk–transcended mere show. First, keep in mind the time frame. The day the obelisk went up was the same day Robert E. Lee was buried at Arlington. Second, remember the Battle of Atlanta, in which General Sherman burned a wide swath of utter ruin to the sea? That went right through this neighborhood. Spent minié balls and Confederate coins still pop up in nearby backyards. Battlefields in the Civil War were not specially designated places away from the lives and homes of civilians. The farming fields, woods, and railroads surrounding this spot were war zone, and at the time a lot more than coins were turning up in people's yards.

Kevin tells me about the principal task taken up by ALMA. The organization gave out boot-sized shoeboxes to people so they could collect soldiers' remains from fields and woodlands. The boxes were so diminutive simply because there wasn't much left of the bodies found years after the war's end. According to one account, "[t]he soldiers had been wrapped in their blankets, face up, hands crossed over their chests and kepi hats covering their faces." In the intervening years, many "had crumbled to dust."[4]

"We actually have a reproduction box somewhere here in the office, and it's quite small, basically just long enough for a femur bone to lie in," says Kevin.

ALMA buried three thousand boxes around a huge sculpture of a dying lion with a look of convulsed grief frozen in its face. It's a replica of Switzerland's Lion of Lucerne. The original sculpture from which this one is modeled commemorates the mercenary Swiss Guard soldiers who died while France's King Louis XVI, Marie Antoinette, and family fled Paris's Tuileries Palace–another lost cause of sorts. Looking at this version of the lion now, and at the smooth lawn surrounding it, I think about all those small boxes buried below. We are both very quiet.

In my paperback guide to Oakland, there are a number of pictures of this place from different decades. Here's the Confederate pillar surrounded by top-hatted gentleman, parasoled ladies, and children pushing hoops and buying snacks from vendors; it all resembles farmland in this newspaper sketch. The next picture shows the pillar during an 1890s Confederate Memorial Day ceremony; a third is from 1950. Last night I tried to trace a single tree from picture to picture, a single building, but the perspective changes just enough so that you can't tell, can't hold the thread. Nothing would stand still the way I wanted it to.

Here at this spot, though, I think of Kevin's story of the little boxes of bones. The small scraps of paper that soldiers would pin to their deceased comrades' blankets, in hope that the men and boys might be found before those scraps disintegrated. How they did disintegrate as the weeks wore on into months, and longer. Some combination of these things, and also Jon's old story about finding two buttons from Civil War uniforms in his own backyard, all work on me, and the experience I sought from all those photos in books arises without my permission. For just a moment, time accordions in on itself. The reason we're here and the moment become one, and my heart is in my mouth for it.

———————

In the grassy field along the cemetery's eastern diagonal, a beautiful German shepherd trots by, accompanied by his owner. There is always a woman with her dogs here, just as there are always runners and people drawing charcoal sketches all over the cemetery. The Historic Oakland Foundation strongly encourages these visitors, in the name of interest, support, money.

The dog woman smiles at us as we stop to scratch the ears of her pup. He leans hard into my hand and proceeds to roll around on his back in the lush, green grass. This was Potters' Field, the approximately seven-and-a-half acre space where the city buried the penniless and unknown dead starting in the mid-1860s.

By the summer of 1864, many of Atlanta's inhabitants had fled the city to escape the violent ruination that war would bring. Just six years later, in the thick of Reconstruction, the population had shot up to twenty-one thousand, more than twice what it had been just a decade prior.

"After the Civil War, a lot of rural people who were destitute came to Atlanta looking for work," says Kevin, who I insist is not a dreary man. "And there were not enough jobs to go around, and so you would have droves of homeless people. And they would be living in squalid conditions and would be victims of crime." Observers of the rebuilding reported that Atlanta was a hive of industry, its red-mud streets "alive from morning to night with carts, barrows, and wagonloads of timber, brick and sand." It was a boomtown, and it developed both the squalor and the lawlessness associated with boomtowns. Many white and recently freed black families lived in government camps in shelters with roofs of "jagged . . . tin sheeting held down by rocks."[5]

At that time, this quiet field was uneven ground dotted with markers crafted from fugitive materials: makeshift plywood or stones or whatever else people had on hand. It's a brutal picture that's hard to reconjure now that the old Potters' Field looks like a triangle of rolling parkland. It's probably safe to say that this was not the cemetery section visited by all those young couples and families in the cemetery's romantic heyday, but if there's any place in Oakland you're likely to see folks picnicking now, it's here.

In this way, Oakland Cemetery resembles nothing so much as a city complete with its own class system. In one neighborhood, you've got the beautiful and tacky high-rise statuary of the wealthy and climbing. You have a whole lot of average middle-class headstones, and then you have spaces like one we ran across in the old African American section just before this: a dingy patch of dirt, with tiny brown rock markers jutting up like broken teeth. And then there are those who get nothing.

The oldest cemetery tells the story of its city in more ways than one. It is significant, for example, that the first body interred here was that of Dr. Nissan the Unknown Transient. When Oakland was founded in 1850, Atlanta was little more than a brash railroad hub. The otherwise sensible and fairly dull website for Georgia's Secretary of State says outright that in these fledgling years, Atlanta was "more saloons than churches; more bawdy houses than banks." The surge in railroad routes had rapidly populated the city with people hoping to improve their lot: Business impresarios. Railroad men. Prostitutes. For years, Atlanta had a lot more in common with the town of Deadwood than with the town of Savannah.

The establishment of a tasteful rural-style cemetery like this one was on par with the opening of the town's first theater, the Athenaeum, four years later. Oakland was the railroad man showing off, donning top hat and tails, trying to establish this money-clogged burg as a place of substance and to further its bid to be made state capital.

That wish was granted in 1868, a time when the city's primary endeavor was rebuilding from the ground up, post-Sherman–inaugurating Atlanta's pattern of continually razing itself to reinvent. Standing in this place amounts not only to observing dead history;

it's witnessing an earlier facelift, one of the first of the city's many attempts to remake itself in the national gaze.

We start back toward the car. A stiff breeze blows across the lawns as we pass the Kiser statue, an eight-foot Romanesque lady who points ominously up at the dark clouds now rolling through the sky. The rain predicted all afternoon feels close, and we pick up our pace, loaded down as we are with paper and small, expensive digital machines.

Mausoleums, those burial vaults that stood as icons of industrial wealth and renown so fashionable in the late nineteenth and early twentieth centuries, perch all over the place here on Oakland's highest hills. I peek into one belonging to the family of J. C. Peck. Even in today's overcast gloom, bright shards of light from a stained-glass window picturing Christ on the cross light up the inside vestibule. As I peer through the bars of the cold, wrought-iron door, taking in the interior hallway with its elegant black-and-white checked floor, marble bench, and wall of stacked burial chambers, a shockingly chill breeze reverberates through the chamber and hits me.

These vaults denoted the ultimate in success and power, but I can't help but feel unnerved and just *sorry* for the people entombed here. There's a vulnerability in how their closed coroner-style drawers are on display for any stranger like me who wants to take a gander.

Something Charles-Foster-Kane lonely, too, about the idea of being stuck inside some ornate granite gargoyled house, even after your own death. So close to the earth, but not united with it. These men, the industrial martyrs in the battle to establish Atlanta as a city of distinction, with their wives and children. It makes me shiver. I cannot keep my eyes from those drawers. You look at them and there is no doubt as to their purpose and contents—and for the first time, the wonder of this place feels like something more than pure history. Cold mortality stirs and says *Hello*. I unclasp my fingers and skip away from here like a child, fast.

———————

The cemetery is one of those subjects that divides people into ideo-
logical camps. Some people hate the memorial parks with the markers made flat so maintenance workers can easily mow right over
them; they call them the worst example of craven, corporate-owned
funeral business. Or they hate mausoleums, or they reserve a special
dislike for cremation.

And then there are people like my dad's mother. Her ashes are
buried at Valley Forge Memorial Gardens near Philadelphia. It's a sedate place. Some of the markers are flush with the ground and some
are not, but the whole thing is ordered and neat, a later iteration of
cemetery. More French garden than English, more golf course than
either. The orderliness gives the place a propriety the rambling acres
at Oakland will never achieve.

By the time my grandmother hit her teens, her father had wrested
the family to a measure of affluence. There were white tablecloths
and servants. Unsurprisingly, a streak of the mannered ran through
my grandmother to the end of her days. I cannot imagine her finding much appealing about Oakland. She was a woman of those generations just following the Victorians, and I know she would hate the
gaudy statues and the broken bricks. I have a mostly rational view of
the world, but if we had laid Jeanne Sweeney's ashes to rest amid this
beautiful, broken tumult, I just know: She would haunt us.

Places like Valley Forge or your local Shady Acres Memorial Park
(whose name I am fabricating; I intend no criticism toward any of the
real Shady Acreses) are logistically more user-friendly than Oakland
ever was, even in its prime, but these successive articulations of the
graveyard did not spring from nothing. Some people may hold up two
examples in opposition, the "old, creepy cemeteries" and the "new,
orderly cemeteries," but the latter would never have existed had it
not been for Oakland. In a way, Oakland was a grandmother, the first
in an evolutionary chain: the cemetery conscious of itself.

And then there are people like Mary Woodlan, who, at one point
in conversation, used the word "love" to describe her feelings for
Oakland no fewer than five times in five minutes. There are societies

and websites and publications like *Epitaphs* magazine, created by and for rabid fans of old boneyards.

But for all the people who think Victorian rural cemeteries, with their riot of monuments and trees, are lovely places, no one is building new ones. Part of the reason has to do with the popularity of cremation and the transience of Americans today. Part of it might also be an effect of income taxes; the wealthy among us can no longer so freely import Italian marble and have workers spend ten years handcrafting a gothic mausoleum.

Really, though, I think the reason no one's building more Oaklands is this: The very quality that endears such places to us is their feel of the ancient and the unknowable. The rural cemetery is the archetypical cemetery, but we've mostly moved on from the Victorian view of death. Today, we tend to think of such places as tourist sites, not as potential spots to spend eternity ourselves.

In that irony inherent in so many things decades past their heyday, Oakland means more to the preservationists of today than it did to the people who buried their dead here while the cemetery was in its prime. Sure, the Victorians put up monuments and held picnics, but they didn't worry constantly about Oakland's cultural and historic importance or plan very well for its future. The cemetery was in decay back in 1976 when the Historic Oakland Foundation commenced its restoration efforts. Its primary goal was to preserve Oakland, not to attract new burials. And I think this is one reason we can stand to visit. Instead of reminding us too much of our own mortality, Oakland makes us think mostly of mythic anecdotes, of history.

And frankly, we like the decay. We enjoy the sense of historical connection here, but we're also attracted to how decrepit it all feels. We like the feeling that we're seeing an endangered piece of the past. How long will that crumbling arch remain that crumbling arch? Lucky we caught it before it became just a pile of rubble. A week after my visit to Oakland, a tornado blew through Atlanta, one of very few in recorded history. As such storms are wont to do, its capricious dance devastated a few neighborhoods and left others untouched. But it ripped through Cabbagetown's blocks of historic shotgun houses, and it also gutted Oakland. Fallen trees and broken monuments crowded walkways and cemetery blocks for weeks after, and the place was closed to visitors for months. The rebuilding process took more than a year. "Rebuilding" means restoring what monuments can be restored and planting new trees. But what's gone is irreparably lost and will never come back.

As the first drops of rain begin to fall, Jon and I continue back toward the entrance and his car, out there waiting for us in the present day. We rush past the marker for Atlanta's first baby (Julia Carlyle Withers, 1842-1919) and the one for Confederate captain William Fuller (1836-1905), who led the capture of the three Yankee spies who had absconded with *The General*, a Confederate locomotive. One block away, the spies were hanged and buried here before being reinterred at the National Cemetery in Chattanooga. We pass a sign pointing the way to Margaret Mitchell's grave and to that of former Atlanta mayor Maynard Jackson, and we almost–but don't quite–miss a non-descript flat marker that I beg Jon to photograph since the battery on my camera's almost dead. The marble stone, small and flush with the weeds and the browning grass on the leaf-littered ground, reads only "This Man Lived."

DISMAL TRADE

Kay Powell,
Obituary Writer

The Doyenne Speaks

The Doyenne of the Death Beat is only five-foot-four and as nice as you please. Her greeting is both warm and sharp when we meet at a hip restaurant she recommended in a trendy Atlanta neighborhood.

"Hello. Kay Powell," she says, shaking my hand and smiling, her voice honeyed with a Georgia accent and oxidized with a lifelong smoker's rough edge. As we sit down together at an outside table, I feel her eyes sizing me up in a way that brings to mind both a seasoned journalist's acumen and certain of my own southern relations. Scrutiny and warmth.

It's a sunny afternoon in 2007. Kay Powell, obituary writer for the *Atlanta Journal-Constitution*, has been working in newsprint for more than thirty years, with one short break, and loves it. She is smart and she is utterly present; if you are not clear, she will ask you what you mean, exactly. Like all good journalists, she is always paying attention. She is looking for the story, the truth, the question behind the question, the good lead.

> *At Matthews Cafeteria, a smiling Thelma Hogan called you by your first name, asked after your mama, made sure your corn bread was cooked just like you liked it and hugged your child in her lap while she rang up your lunch on the cash register.*
> *She did that about 800 times a day for 43 years.*
>
> (Monday, May 28, 2007)

A fan of Powell's named Thomas Hobbs bestowed the "Doyenne" moniker. Some ten years before, another fan, named Carolyn Gilbert, had started the Great Obituarists' Conference, a popular annual gathering for people who write about the dead and people who love to read about them. At one of these conferences, Hobbs, an archivist at the University of South Carolina, approached Kay Powell.

"And he started quoting whole paragraphs from my obits," she tells me, between sips of iced tea. "I said, 'How do you know that story? How do you know that obit?' And that's when he told me he'd been archiving them. For years."

Hobbs was not alone. Neither was he unhealthily obsessed–at least, no more so than your average devoted fan. In her 2006 book, *The Dead Beat: Lost Souls, Lucky Stiffs, and the Perverse Pleasures of Obituaries*, Marilyn Johnson wrote that journalist-written obituaries and their admirers were part of a cultural movement, and that the form was seeing a renaissance of sorts. It's a movement that might have started with Jim Nicholson of the *Philadelphia Daily Inquirer*. A seasoned investigative journalist, Nicholson first provoked shakes of the head from colleagues in the 1980s when he relocated to his paper's obit desk, a beat then considered proverbial pastureland for about-to-retirees and young greenhorns getting their first taste of newspaper work. Nicholson, however, exploded this perception. His well-written life portraits of schoolteachers, letter carriers, and other noncelebrities won attention and accolades–including, in 1987, the first award from the American Society of News Editors (ASNE) given to an obit writer. (Tom Shales and Alana Baranick went on to receive ASNE Awards for their obits in 1988 and 2005.)

In the years since, the humble obit has been anthologized, Pulitzer-Prized, and made the star of scores of quirky articles, scholarly articles, and everything in between. A 2002 study by Northwestern University even recommended that newspapers seeking to increase readership cover "community announcements, obituaries, [and] stories about ordinary people."[1] Kay Powell calls people who actively read obituaries and trade and discuss them online "fobits." That's short for Friends of Obits.

As for those who write them: In the 1990s and first decade of the twenty-first century, the death beat became the coveted province of outstanding journalists like Adam Bernstein of the *Washington Post*; Jim Sheeler, who won a Pulitzer for his obits in the *Rocky Mountain News*; and Kay Powell herself.

She began her career as the city editor at the *Valdosta Times* in the 1970s. Early on, between cranking out gritty, award-winning reports on child abuse, incest, substandard housing, and discrimination, she also wrote the more formulaic obituary notices. But it was the details that didn't show up in print that captivated her. "I was the one who was always, 'Oh, my gosh! She was so young! What'd she die of? And what are all those children gonna do?'"

When we think of obituary pages written by the pros, bios of the rich and publicly acclaimed dead come to mind, those stories that splash a life's worth of details and photos across the eminent pages of papers like the *New York* and *L.A. Times*. But Powell's paper, the *Atlanta Journal-Constitution*, grants some ordinary joes the same detailed profile-and-photo treatment that celebrities get at other papers. "I'm writing about everyday people walking the streets," says Powell with a preemptive trace of impatience. "And love doing it.

"And while every other reporter is doing their fifteenth or twentieth weather story? Or first day of school or city council or, you know, routine crime, if there is such a thing? I'm getting to tell a different *life*–Thank you." This to the waiter who has finally brought her a requested ashtray. "–a different story that *changes*. Every. Single. Day." And there are always surprises, she notes, before turning away politely to exhale from her first drag. "I mean, I don't know. Today is it gonna be the King of the Gypsies? Is it gonna be Thelma Hogan from the cafeteria? I don't know. And I sure have fun finding out and deciding who to write on."

(A note: Regular paid death notices written by family members still exist, of course. Kay considers these to be a form of modern folk art, and she's memorized her all-time favorite, from the *Valdosta Times*: "On Wednesday, November 19th, 1996, God saw fit for Brother Marslone, Senior, to tell him all about it.")

Every eight-hour shift he worked at Delta Air Lines, Mike Huddleston was responsible for getting 5,000 pieces of luggage to the correct spot at Hartsfield International Airport. . . . Even after a work accident cost Mr. Huddleston two fingers, and two more were reattached, he remained a positive employee, said [his supervisor, Bruce] Smith.

"He was hooking a trailer up to a baggage tug, and there was a brake failure in the baggage tug," said his supervisor. "From that point on, his nickname was 'Nub.'"

(Monday, September 22, 2003)

In a city whose metro population tops five million, how does a staff of two decide whose death matters enough for print? "It is *the* worst part of my day," says Kay, and this is the only superlative she uses during our entire conversation. She is a careful speaker. "If you figure we get forty-five to sixty or more deaths a day, and we can only write on one person, I hate having to make those decisions; I hate it."

But in the end, she's on deadline, and time is limited. So she asks questions: Have they told a story like this before? When is the funeral? How many phone calls would she have to place? Once the decision is made, there's no second-guessing. The clock's running and the phone calls start. For time's sake, Kay does all her work by phone. The story must print before the funeral; that usually means she has five or six hours to go from Name and Cause of Death to a six-hundred-word encapsulation that will make readers feel like they know the deceased well. So Kay is calling family members who are at the funeral home, or at the cemetery picking out a plot, or at the mall finding a black slip to go with a dress, or picking up out-of-town relatives from the airport. "I have talked to women sittin' under the hair drier." She's thankful for the invention of the cell phone. How many phone calls does she usually make per story? "Oh, Lord. You can make a dozen, or you can make thirty.

"And yes, it's sad, and yes, it's tragic—but you're a professional. You've got a job to do! And I'm not hard-hearted by any means. It's just that I know I'm gonna write a good story, and I know it's gonna accurately reflect that person's life."

To make sure that happens, she calls a lot of people. Nephews, cousins, family friends. She asks them what Aunt Elizabeth did once that surprised them. She does *not* ask what Grandpa Jim's hobbies were. Instead, she might ask—and this voice is butter-smooth in the asking—'When he had a little time to himself, that he could just go and do what was fun for *Jim* to do, what would he do? The thing that made him feel better afterwards?'

"And they might say, 'Well, you know, one weekend Mama and I had been out of town, and when we came back, our house was just filled with all these little exquisite clay sculptures of figurines! And we never even knew that he had an interest!'"

In a finished story, this beats "He liked hunting."

Everything had to be just so for Edith Adams: forming a line, seating at meals, her appearance and answering "Jeopardy!" questions.

"She was real stubborn. She knew her own mind. We had to fight her to take her car away at 91," said her niece Judy Elrod of Atlanta. "She just wanted it her way all the time. She had a very strong will."

(Wednesday, September 12, 2007)

She's nowhere until she has a good lead. Midafternoon, Kay will sit and look at her notes—all written in longhand on a small legal pad, underlined and starred and marked up with notes in the margins. "I tried, at first, taking them on the computer, and people could hear me [typing] on the phone and it intimidated them." She'll go outside for a cigarette to pace and think, but until she has her lead, she can't write a thing.

She's smoking a cigarette now, not gesturing with it but holding it utterly still with her far hand, the right one, as she speaks, relaxed now. Rather than an accessory, the cigarette seems an object so customary it would be more of a surprise to find it absent than present.

"A lot of people write and then just go back and work on the lead, but the lead, to me, is like the coat hanger. And it truly has to be what draws people in."

Her favorite lead she's ever written: "George Hopkins died again, Friday." Mr. Hopkins had tested deep-sea diving equipment during World War II, and on one such test, the equipment failed and he suffocated and was pronounced dead. However, he was then resuscitated and lived some sixty more years, only to die for good at the age of eighty-three. Then there was the humorist and oxymoron expert. Kay's lead: "The novice, master, national, local authority and internationally unknown expert of oxymorons, former Georgia State professor Warren S. Blumenfeld, died of colon cancer Wednesday." She wrote an obit for Pluto (1930–2006) when its status was downgraded to dwarf planet. "Pluto, the least of the major celestial bodies, never asked to be a planet." The story ends with: "Survivors include eight planets, Earth, Jupiter, Mars, Mercury, Neptune, Saturn, Uranus and Venus."

Her favorite obit headline of all time is not one she wrote, but one that appeared a few years ago in the *New York Post*. A beloved community elder was holding her hundredth birthday party. Just as friends were wheeling out her candle-laden cake, she had a fatal heart attack. The headline? "It's My Party and I'll Die if I Want To."

Kay credits her success both to her reporter's training and instinct and to her upbringing in Valdosta, Georgia. "I know how to talk to 'em." To some extent, Kay feels for her subjects. However, the finished product, the obituary, is not *for* the family. It's for her readers. It's for journalism. Each and every day, she calls brand-new widows and grieving parents in their very darkest stages of living to extract from them the most beloved and reviled traits of the person they're mourning.

Some are more willing to talk than others. Her very toughest case was that of a former Ku Klux Klan honcho named Calvin Craig. Craig had undergone a very public transformation in the late 1960s, garnering national press attention when he gave up his Grand Dragon post to work on voter registration and housing reform with civil rights activist Xernona Clayton. In the years after that particular spotlight faded, Craig proceeded to establish a second white supremacy group. When he died, it took Kay a morning of lengthy phone calls to convince both his wife and his son to talk with her for the obit. "In fact," she says, "when I got through with my conversation, I got a standing ovation by the newsroom!" While she can't recall exactly what she said in those phone calls to convince the man's family to talk, she does say that an hour after the original negotiations, the son called back to tell her he still was not sure; he just wanted to make sure her portrayal was fair. "I couldn't handle it any other way," she told him. The obit went forward.

She gets lied to nearly every day. "And a lot of times, it's not a deliberate lie. What we have are those family myths passed down that everyone believes." She checks every claim and turns up a surprising number of falsehoods: about the supposed war veteran who may or may not actually have seen active duty, or the minor-league baseball star who wasn't. One of Kay's go-to men is an expert on Atlanta's former minor league team, the Crackers. When one family sent her photos of their patriarch wearing a Crackers uniform, her source took a look at the photo and said, "No. That man tried out for us one summer, but he didn't make the team." Family legend.

She's especially careful of superlatives, of people claiming that someone was the first person to do something, or the last living anything. "Any '-est' word, you have to watch out for. First, last, only; it must be confirmed. 'Cause I can guarantee you, the minute you use one, you're gonna hear from fifteen families saying, 'No, my daddy was the first. My mama was the first.'"

Then there are the obit clichés. "Oh, my god," she says, and takes a deep drag on her cigarette. Then exhales the following: "'He was a Renaissance man,' 'She was a true southern belle,' 'Battled cancer,' 'Never met a stranger,' 'He'd give you the shirt off his back.' And Jim Sheeler? Who wrote for the *Rocky Mountain News*? When people told him someone would give you the shirt off his back, he'd say, 'Oh? When did you see him do that?'"

Kay has a sign on her desk that says *God is my assignment editor*. There is an unnamable eeriness inherent in her career. What about the fact that absolutely no one she features has an inkling of it the morning before? And is it true that celebrities die in threes?

"Well, we've got that," says Kay drily. "We'll have, sometimes, Dead Lawyer Week, Dead Teacher Week, Dead Preacher Week. . . . And it's not uncommon for a spouse to die within six months of the other spouse." She shrugs. "But I don't know. That 'Dying in Threes,' I don't know about that."

It's just journalism, she says, refusing to entertain any larger implications. Does she feel the weight of responsibility for shaping the general public's remembrance of a person?

"No," she says. "If you think about that, then you're gonna start manipulating the story. I go back to what I said originally: You tell a true story honestly. And you don't manipulate. We don't go for the pathos."

In one way, this level of exchange is slightly disappointing, but it's reflexively comforting, too: Who, after all, would choose a midwife who got all misty about the miracle of life while you or your wife were in the throes of labor? A surgeon who paused in the midst of surgery to think, *My god, I'm holding a beating human heart*? "If you tell a true story honestly," says Kay, "if you aren't judgmental–I mean, it takes all the good reporter skills. It just so happens the person's dead."

David Robeson Morgan was a brilliant man whose future looked good, until he had a frontal lobotomy in 1947. After a life of alcoholism and menial jobs, he found redemption in science. . . . He donated his body to Emory so the research could continue after he died Wednesday at Henry Medical Center of complications following hip surgery.

It gave meaning to the ordeal of his life, said his brother, Neil Morgan of San Diego.

(Saturday, May 27, 2000)

While her stories are in no way a service to the surviving relatives–an obit about a disbarred lawyer will state that fact flat out–Kay says families do treasure the final written piece. Most leap at the opportunity to talk with her. "One thing I never would have expected," she says. "It's when people say we helped them through their grieving by talking to them, and by listening to them talk." People photocopy her obits. Give them out at funerals. Blow them up and display them on easels at the service. Laminate them. Bury them with the person who died. Send them all over the world. "I get letters from Saudi Arabia and Japan and Ireland."

At the end of the day, what satisfies Kay Powell? "I met deadline." Without pause, she says this, a note of contention in her voice. *We don't go for the pathos.* Then, another of those arid looks. She stubs out her cigarette, pauses, says, "I told one of my editors one night, 'Look, Laura, I've got to have more room. I've gone and fallen in love with this man,' and she said, 'Kay, you fall in love with all of 'em. You've got to start fallin' in love with 'em while they're still *alive.*'" She cracks a smile. Her laugh, when it happens, is both smoky and contagious.

REVEALED:

The fall and rise of
a dying form

CHAPTER FOUR

The Last Great
Obit Writers' Conference

The reason for the very first printed death announcements might have been nothing more than raw necessity. Marilyn Johnson, who wrote an entire book on the recent resurgence of the obituary, tells me that it's possible the modern obit's eldest traceable great-ancestor showed up during England's Black Death. "You know," she says, "when people nailed lists of the dead to tavern doors to let everyone know that their drinking buddies had died." An Australian scholar named Nigel Starck traced the first English-language obituary back to a 1620 ancestor of the modern newspaper, which ran a chronicle of the life and death of one Captain Andrew Shilling under the snappy title, "The True Relation of That Worthy Sea Fight Which two of the East India Shipps had with 4 Portugals, of great force, and burthen, in the Persian Gulph."[1]

About a hundred years later on this side of the Atlantic, colonial presses fashioned beautiful, though ghoulish, broadsides to com-

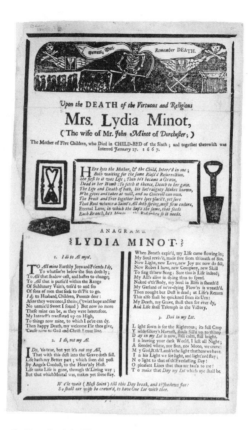

Upon the Death of the Virtuous and Religious Mrs. Lydia Minot.
Broadside, Cambridge, Massachusetts, Samuel Green, 1668.

memorate the dead. These poster-sized sheets often featured the sermons that had been spoken over coffins, and they were not limited to social luminaries either; broadsides were made up for man, woman, and child. A 1710 broadside, bordered in skulls, crossbones, and full skeletons, tells the story of one "amiable virgin," six-year-old Rebekah Sewall. It reads, in part, "I saw no Place Secure; but all must dy. / Death, that stern Officer, takes no denial[.]"[2] While not quite the encapsulation of a specific life attempted by later obituaries, the broadside's cheery imagery, and certainly its text, demonstrated the God-takes-no-prisoners view of life and death so insistent in Puritan thinking.

A century later, early national news publications like the *Niles Weekly Register* and the *National Intelligencer* were publishing life details in their obituaries. And while the broadsides of the early 1700s had concentrated on the religious devotion of the departed, these accounts detailed a new set of desirable qualities. Rugged love of country, for example, was the central feature of one 1818 obit headed "Another Revolutionary Patriot Gone!" Seventy-eight-year-old John Chestnutt "was distinguished by his zeal and patriotism in the service of his country throughout the revolutionary war, and contributed not a little to the success of the eventful struggle for American Independence."[3]

By 1870, the genre revealed a new American definition of a life worth recognizing: affluence and professional success.[4] Prominent dailies like the *New-York Daily Times* (later the *New York Times*) and the *New Orleans Picayune* ran both news obituaries penned by journalists and family-written death notices. A typical example of the former is the obit for "Hero of Commerce" Mark Walton, a man whose "life was one of continued devotion to business. . . . He was abstemious, regular and industrious in habits, an early riser, steady, thoughtful and methodical. . . . Every step of his long and meritorious career was marked with generous deeds."[5]

During this time, women and minorities were, unsurprisingly, the subjects of few obituaries compared to men of status like Walton, and when they were featured, their highlighted attributes were those that supported the status quo—for example, the Native American who aided the white man in battle, or the loyal wife whose most rewarding work took place in her home.[6] Twelve percent of the obits in the *Niles Weekly Register* for 1818 were for women. By 1930 women were the subject of 32 percent of the *San Francisco Chronicle*'s obits.[7] Keenly aware of decades of exclusion, today's obituary columns the nation over are actively endeavoring to seek out territory beyond that of the dead, white male.

In a genre whose occasion for existence is always the same, the question of who merits mention becomes paramount. In our nation's early days, it was the pioneers and Revolutionary heroes; later on, successful businessmen. Today, when our espoused values are more egalitarian, the genre has expanded far beyond the province of the Mark Waltons of the world. Now, journalists are writing obits about middle-class waterskiing fiends, homeless men, even three-year-olds. One question besets today's obit writer wherever she goes: If everyone is qualified to have his or her entire life committed, for all time, to black ink on newsprint or pixels on screen, then who merits such treatment? If the death-beat writer haunts the Grim Reaper's every move, then it is this question that, in turn, stalks her.

Carolyn Gilbert is a little obsessed with obituaries. She and some friends used to meet regularly but informally to exchange and discuss their favorites that they'd clipped and collected from newspapers around the country, from the *Atlanta Journal-Constitution*, the *Denver* and *Washington Post*s, and other papers that were printing stories of the famous, infamous, and heretofore unknown newly deceased. It was partly on a dare in 1999 that Carolyn formed the International Association of Obituarists, the first organization to recognize obituary writers as a distinct group of professionals, and to recognize them as fans do: as creatures akin to demigods.

She was a bit surprised when her inaugural gathering, the First Great Obituarist Conference, attracted dozens of the writers she and her friends admired from all over this country and several others. (Canadian and British publications are widely considered titans of the genre–namely, Toronto's *Globe and Mail* for its well-written, and lengthy, obits on ordinary citizens, and the *Daily Telegraph* for its excellent obituaries of a wide range of celebrities.) And because Carolyn was not a writer herself–she's an event planner from Texas–she invited other aficionados of the death beat, too. The resulting gathering sounds something like Dragon*Con, the yearly convention where science fiction and fantasy writers mingle with devotees who arrive dressed up like Klingons or Xena, Warrior Princess. Only this is an entire weekend for obituarists.

Yes, it's made up, that word. An "obituarist" is someone who proudly appreciates the craft on an obsessive level, who pens accounts of the dead or who, like Carolyn, subscribes to three of four newspapers and scans the internet to read about the latest dead each day.

I accidentally learn about the conference because it would be impossible not to. Positively everything I read about the State of the Obituaries Today mentions scenes from nine years of Great Conferences: The time two attendees pulled up to the hotel in a hearse painted blue and green. The year a British newsman held court, sporting a ten-gallon hat and a margarita. Or the year someone showed up dressed like the Grim Reaper. Carolyn reigns at the center of the swirl, always, housemother and fan of this genre that's finally being celebrated in suitable eccentric splendor.

Little do I realize it, but this year's Great Obituarist Conference signals an apex of a moment in history that is already fleeting. Or maybe one tick of the clock just past it. In 2008, the Great gatherings parallel the egalitarian feel of the modern death beat. It's a time when you're nearly as likely to come across journalist-penned obits about the quirky un-famous as you are to read about the lives of the long renowned. At this conference, the stars of this genre mix with the hoi polloi, and everyone sits together at the same conference table.

And anyone can attend. Sort of. One criterion that can be a little trying is that you've got to be willing to travel. Every year, Carolyn intentionally chooses an off-the-beaten-track location for her conferences, way-out little burgs like Alfred, New York, or Bath, England. Towns without airports. It comes down to Carolyn's dogged reverse-snobbery. She calls her locations "intimate." They foster a closeness among attendees, she says, that you could not replicate in a major metropolitan conference center. For the last several years an average of thirty to forty devotees have taken vacation days and traveled to these strange locales, all for an unbroken weekend devoted to meeting up with fellow obsessives to discuss the craft, style, and latest trends of a genre so specific that none of its subjects will ever see their own stories.

This year's the tenth anniversary.

So of course I have to go.

Two featured speakers at this year's conference are Kay Powell, the *Atlanta Journal-Constitution* reporter, and Jim Sheeler, the Pulitzer Prize winner who first made his name by writing intimate, precise life profiles for the *Rocky Mountain News*. The presence of both Powell and Sheeler is sure to attract fans. I've read about these fans. In years past, they've packed readings and panel discussions, bringing spouses, wanting autographs, and getting just as involved as the writers in the discussions that follow.

Kay Powell loves this. She's made good friends with Tom Hobbs, the obits enthusiast and librarian whom she met when she overheard him at a previous conference quoting whole passages of her stories aloud. Fans like Hobbs, says Kay, "make us feel like rock stars." Well, then, rock on, Kay. Let's go to Vegas.

Las Vegas, New Mexico, has little in common with its famous besequined and pneumaticized counterpart one state over. The larger Las Vegas's conceit lies in its feats of self-transformation: an artificial New York skyline cheek-by-jowl with a miniature Eiffel Tower.

Las Vegas, New Mexico, is a sleepy corner of a different sort of legend. The Santa Fe Trail once meandered through here, and Wyatt Earp, Doc Holiday, and Billy the Kid are said to have passed many an evening in the town's old Plaza Hotel, which is hosting the conference. And while the big Las Vegas is an explosive dynamo that can be seen from space, Las Vegas, New Mexico, doesn't have an airport. What it does have is extraordinarily unaffected Old West charm. By "extraordinarily unaffected," I mean that it's the kind of place locals will stop and chat with you in the town square about how pleased they are that you're enjoying your visit. More than once. A lot of residents seem proud of this place, proud that portions of *Easy Rider* were filmed here, and that in *No Country for Old Men*, Josh Brolin and Javier Bardem stalked each other right here in the lobby of the Plaza.

The night I arrive, the airy, oaken lobby does look like a setting straight out of a cowboy movie—save for the mood, which is brisk and giddy and centered about a bright, zaftig woman seated at a small round table across from the front desk. Clad in warm reds and purples, she is readjusting her reading glasses as she introduces people to one another. I watch her unite an obit writer from southern New Mexico with a librarian from Berkeley. A British fan who's filming a documentary on obits with a high school teacher from Arizona. Another attendee is an anthropologist, researching obituaries for pets. It's the makings for a really interesting cocktail hour for complete nerds, and soon I am caught up.

"Why, hello!" says the bright woman, who is, of course, Carolyn Gilbert. She knows who I am immediately. Her words are made even friendlier by the warm Texas accent elongating her vowels. She introduces me, with a full bio, to Larken Bradley, an obit writer from California, and we shake hands. As Carolyn makes sure I have a cocktail and tells me to make a name tag for myself, I am reminded of certain English teachers of my youth, the ones who were always wearing shoes from different pairs by mistake and making loud fun of themselves for it, the ones magnanimous in their praise for torturous love poetry written by fifteen-year-olds. They looked at you, and you felt they knew your secret best thing.

Before she started up the International Association of Obituarists in 1999, Carolyn Gilbert was, in fact, a high school English teacher, but that job's routine structure rankled her, and she quit to do event planning. There's no doubt she's in her element here, holding her margarita aloft as she stokes the social fire.

It's a moment that represents, absolutely, this conference's sparkly, unpretentious spirit—because if Carolyn Gilbert has an allergy, it's to people and organizations who take themselves too seriously. Her grip on the reins of the Greats is at once fierce and light: What happens, who speaks and when, is subject to her own rescheduling and sense of spontaneity. She loves the story about the year the obit fans showed up in the blue and green hearse. And she does not shy from the darkest humor, like calling a lyric passage from a writer like Jim Sheeler "drop-dead genius prose," smirking to acknowledge the pun the second before her expression goes earnest to underscore that she really means it.

My favorite story about the Greats is from the third conference in Bath, England. That's when Hugh Massingberd, a renowned wit of the obit world and journalist from the *London Daily Telegraph*, spoke. Carolyn starts telling me this story. Then Kay Powell overhears and joins in, and soon others come up to listen. Hugh Massingberd is often called the "father of the modern British obituary," and they tell this story now as if his appearance at a conference represented some holy manifestation. This might be due, in part, to Massingberd's own death from cancer last year. In his *New York Times* obituary, Margalit Fox called him the man "who made a once-dreary page required reading by speaking frankly, wittily and often gleefully ill of the dead."[8]

So, Massingberd was taking the train from London to grace the Third Great, and Carolyn Gilbert wanted to express appreciation. Weeks before, she had come up with the Hall of Fame Award and charged a Dallas journalist named Spencer Michlin with engraving a small crystal monument. Michlin handed it to her just before she spoke a few pithy words at the ceremonial moment. She was holding the award out to the great man when a smoky voice with a southern accent, that just might have belonged to Kay Powell, called out from the back of the room, "Read it out loud! Read it out loud!" Gilbert nodded, looked down at the prize for the first time, and read to all those gathered what she saw there:

International Association of Obituarists

First Hall of Fame Award

I Am Wearing No Underpants.

There was a real award besides, but Kay Powell says, "I think that one captured the spirit of the group."

Such hijinks seem less likely this year, I think, looking around this first night of the Tenth Great. It's not that this crowd strikes me as lifeless; it's just that I'm not convinced of the comparative hell-raising potential of just over a dozen mostly librarians and school-teachers. I've been here for about an hour. I've met the documentary makers, listened to a few of Kay Powell's stories of conferences past, and talked Victorian funerals with the obit writer from North Carolina. Now I notice that the faces around the room aren't accumulating in number. After hearing the legends, and after months of telling people, "I am going to a conference of obituary writers this summer," I am experiencing a slight sinking sensation. During a moment when she's free, I grab Carolyn. She tells me: Yep, this is it. Everyone's here.

This year there will not be thirty or forty people. A grand total of fourteen of us hold cocktails and chat in this Old West saloon. The Tenth Annual Great Obituarists' Conference has begun, and we are it.

It's not like I walked into this blind. Before coming, I talked to people on the phone and lurked on blog pages. I knew that just a few weeks back, a brand-new group had convened another, brand-new gathering that some here are calling "the rival conference." The new group is called the Society of Professional Obituary Writers, or SPOW, and its conference up in Portland was designated Professionals Only. No librarians. No schoolteacher fans. I'm still surprised, though, by the seeming impact here. It's been a half hour, and I've met and spoken with absolutely everyone. Suddenly, the soaring elevation of Las Vegas, New Mexico, and the seventeen-hour travel day behind me hits hard, and I have to set down my half-finished beer and wipe my forehead. Whatever I was expecting, it's going to be a different kind of weekend.

It turns out there are actually some advantages to such a small group. My primary question regarding the weekend, namely, *What kind of people come to a conference devoted to writing about the dead?* is answered right away, when the first session the next morning turns out to be one long getting-to-know-you forum.

Lexy Chubrich is a slim, blonde high school teacher from Arizona possessed of a quick vivacity. Her obit-reading habit started the way many such habits do: at a job she hated. She was spending her days at the local library supposedly summarizing medical studies, but she ended up mostly reading the newspaper instead, particularly the obits. She was entranced by these stories, by how surprising and sad or funny they were, and how well written. Although her mother was going through a terminal illness at the time, Chubrich says that this had nothing to do with her obit fixation. "It's the love of reading and the love of language," she says. "It's fresh and it's immediate."

For Larken Bradley, the obit writer from California, it started earlier. As the daughter of a gravedigger, she says, "I just remember dangling my feet into that ever-deepening hole." She likes to imagine that her work here on earth keeps the Almighty from whisking her off too soon. "You know: He needs me around to write these stories. 'Don't take me yet!'"

The British filmmaker says she studies obits in part to counteract her recurring attacks of nocturnal death terrors, which continue to seize her even in adult life. And a librarian from Berkeley says just the opposite: She has always felt completely comfortable with death, having witnessed her share of sickness and funerals in her childhood as the daughter of a small-town minister. "I never felt like I was a voyeur; I just liked knowing lots of details about lots of different people."

Tom Hobbs, the librarian friend of Kay Powell, has racked up more years at this conference than anyone except Gilbert, having attended every one but the first. He says that the best thing about the Greats is how laid back they are. "It's not some group of high-powered journalists all up in your face." Instead, it's a three-day conversation, one in which a London reporter sits at the same table as a librarian from South Carolina. Or at least it has been like that, every year until now.

When Carolyn breaks us for lunch, it's with a formality that makes me feel a bit sorry, since this group would fit easily at two tables in any restaurant. I find myself conjuring up what this conference must have been like in years past, with dozens of fans and writers. Two weeks before, an obit writer who isn't here told me on the phone that if she were me, she'd wait till next year and go instead to the pros' conference. She would come to this one for a "general, storytelling sort of gathering," but, she said, it wasn't a real assembly of professionals.

Any club based on shared personal passion develops factions. When that personal passion involves a subject that inspires gravity, politeness, and hushed voices–say, *death*–you might imagine those factions treating conflict with a certain deliberate restraint and care. It turns out the opposite is true. It turns out, the gloves come off.

Considering all the forms an obituary takes across the country–a few clerk-scribbled lines citing a funeral's whereabouts, or fawning cliché filler in the back of a pastel section called "Accents" or "Lifestyles"–it's no wonder that good journalistic obit writers, the ones who write concise, unbiased accounts and check their facts, bristle at the idea that what they do somehow lacks merit. Past conference years, for example, saw verbal sparring when writers of the longer-established obits for the famous called into question the import and substance of obits for the average joe. I do not envy the journalist who chose to challenge Kay Powell in such a debate.

Accordingly, a few of this year's writers look a bit tight-lipped when a Friday afternoon session concerning pet obituaries kicks off. The presenter is not an obit writer herself. Rather, anthropologist Jane Desmond is writing a book about human-animal relations. Increasing numbers of profiles of renowned animals are showing up, she tells the group, in a newspaper section "once reserved for the wealthy and powerful white man."

Are such obits merited? she asks. Should a profile of some man's canine best friend appear alongside that of someone else's real best friend? What if that Labrador retriever was a Seeing Eye dog that performed Lassie-like feats of bravery? Or belonged to the president? And if that's permissible, someone else wonders, why stop at animals? What about an obituary for the town's oldest tree, felled by a lightning strike? What about extinguished rivers, which are always disappearing here in the American Southwest?

Throughout this discussion, journalist Kay Powell has been sitting, her eyes flinty and impatient, and now she interjects, "We *do* those stories. They're called features, they're a one-time thing, and they *don't* go on the obit page."

It's touchy, this question of whose life story gets to be a Life Story that gets written and fact-checked and printed on thousands of newspapers. Its answer resonates to depths a lot deeper than Fido versus Aunt Bea. It makes you start to think a lot about who gets a story, period. A neuroscientist named Dave Eagleman recently wrote a decidedly nonscientific book positing forty imaginative versions of the afterlife, or "afterlives," as he puts it. At the start of one chapter, Eagleman writes, "There are three deaths. The first is when the body ceases to function. The second is when the body is consigned to the grave. The third is that moment, sometime in the future, when your name is spoken for the last time."[9]

One of the purposes of memorialization is to prolong that third death for as long as possible. As long as people are talking about you, after all, you're not really erased from human existence. But who, most often, do we choose to remember? Who are today's versions of the memorable industrialist capitalists and heroic housewives of yesteryear? And who are we willing to forget just a little bit sooner?

I remember flipping on my computer to read that the last surviving American soldier to march into Buchenwald concentration camp and witness the horrors there had died. Surely I want to hear his story. How does such an experience affect a man? But we also enjoy reading about people who didn't encounter history writ large, people whose compelling personalities resound within us and make us think. Even if they're, well, assholes. Jim Sheeler, formerly of the *Rocky Mountain News*, wrote eloquently of the life of an intellectual curmudgeon of a homeless man named Severin Foley, a man who, according to his only friend, "'alienated just about everyone he ever met, except maybe me.'"[10]

Who gets a story? Many obit writers won't write about dead infants. In a day when two dozen city denizens die, writers choose the one who demonstrates the most captivating, developed character. Then there's writer Claire Martin. She spent five of her twenty-five years at the *Denver Post* writing obits, and she didn't shy away from writing stories about kids, babies, or even miscarried or premature infants.

For the story of Javant'e Shade, born after only twenty-four weeks' gestation, Claire wrote, "The hum and pulse of the machines and tubes keeping Javant'e alive, so strange during the first week or so, became familiar to his visitors. They flinched whenever he was stuck with a needle for an IV or blood test, and they longed to cradle him. But his skin was as fragile as a moth's wing. Even the softest touch could tear it, exposing veins thin as an eyelash."[11] Claire talks to me later about this story. She says she got calls from people who had experienced miscarriages, who thanked her for acknowledging their

loss and their grief as real. "Whenever I wrote about a baby or someone with disabilities, I heard back from people who said, 'Thank you,
because we feel ignored.'"

We shouldn't downplay the countless hours parents spend speculating about the personalities lying dormant inside their infants and
infants-to-be, says Claire. Nor can we deny the sparks of personality
that *are* displayed—a four-year-old's fixation on wooden puzzles or
a toddler who takes to hiding his diaper under couch cushions. The
moments we mourn and wish to memorialize are as small as these.

I think back to the day I spent with a group of families paying their
respects out on the Atlantic with the company Eternal Reefs, which
turns cremated ashes into artificial coral reefs. The company invites
families to come along on the voyages in which the "reef balls" are
placed on the ocean floor. One couple on this weekend's voyage were
memorializing their cat, Mistofeles. Also remembered that day: a father who had been a lifelong seafarer, a husband who had been a military hero, and a wife who had scuba-dived in the Galapagos while in
her eighties. No matter their résumé-style achievements, all of them
had been people who had influenced hundreds of others in ways large
and small, known and unknown throughout their lifetimes, people
harboring distinct interior universes that had vanished once they
breathed their last.

When I asked their survivors what they thought about the presence of the cat, the response was a uniform polite, nodding acceptance. Maybe nobody wanted to be the jerk who ruined the day's
mood by dissing the pet owners. However, in those actual ceremonial moments when the reef balls honoring the human dead were re-
leased, the deck was crowded with respectful observers. By contrast,
many saw the moment Mistofeles's memorial was dropped as a good
time for a trip inside the cabin for a snack and a chat with relatives.
They were generally polite, but they did not rush to embrace the couple who had traveled from California to the east coast for a cat's memorial service.

When we memorialize someone in print or in ceremony, we don't just record the relationship that was there; we define it for the ages. The first printed obit acknowledging someone's gay partner was a form of ratification. Fido's picture in the paper, next to Frank Sinatra's, next to your father's, doesn't just say that all of these lives were important and appreciated; it grants them all a place at the exact same table.

Which brings us back to this conference table, one year earlier. In her popular online *Obituary Forum*, Alana Baranick had previewed last year's conference this way: "The Numbered Greats are always the highlight of the year for obituary writers and enthusiasts. We make our reservations and pay registration fees often without knowing who will be making presentations or what their topics will be. The fact is, we love getting together with our fellow grimsters. The Great Obituary Writers confabs are more like class reunions than structured seminars." Along with affection, there's a note of something else lurking in that entry, a something that reads like foreshadowing when you know what came next.

The big buzz at last year's "confab" in Alfred, New York, was the location-to-be of this year's conference: Toronto. For the first time ever, a Great was tentatively slated for a nontiny town. A group of journalists from that city's paper, the *Globe and Mail*, were supposed to host, and just after the Ninth Great Conference ended, they began an email correspondence with Carolyn. That's when the trouble began.

Carolyn starts the story this way: "If I had to write my own obituary, I would write, 'She was fun. And spontaneous.' And the 'spontaneous' part sometimes gets me into trouble."

A few attendees had voiced discontent about the previous year's presentation by the Apron Lady, a drop-in attendee named EllynAnne Geisel. Her lecture about the domestic garment as historical document struck some as off-topic. And then there was the town elder whom Carolyn met in the lodge's bar on the first night of the conference. The octogenarian was thrilled to learn about the Great gathering; he had in fact collected his own town's obits for years, and Carolyn was so charmed that she put him on the last day's program. Some attendees were less charmed. One journalist from Toronto was among them.

Following adjournment of the Ninth, *Globe and Mail* editor Colin Haskin wrote to Carolyn. If his city was to host, he said, he needed complete control of the next gathering. "The tenth anniversary conference cannot proceed in the same manner as those in the past," he wrote in an email. There would be no eleventh-hour schedule changes or last-minute guest speakers. He and a lot of others wanted a real newspaper conference worthy of a shining genre that had finally come into its own. In other words, they wanted an entirely different event. In the words of the *Boston Globe*'s Alex Beam's gleefully titled story, "Grave Schism on the Death Beat," the Canadians wanted the Greats to resemble "a real journalists' convention, i.e. boring."[12]

It didn't take long for the mood to turn ugly between Carolyn and the Canadians. Of Colin Haskin, Carolyn says, "He's nothing if not *un*-fun and *un*-spontaneous." In a recent email exchange I had with Colin, he wrote of Carolyn, "She was likeable enough on our first meeting, but that was about as far as it went. She seemed to always to have an agenda separate from anything to do with obituary writing and, for another, had not served so much as a single day in journalism."

In one particularly unpleasant exchange, she facetiously offered to sell him "the entire franchise" for $200,000, choosing the figure because it was the amount she owed on her mortgage.

Colin remembers this differently. "I was astonished, but realized she was serious," he wrote. "She began telling how much money was to be made in selling memberships to obit writers all over the world. Finally, I laughed and told her that very few journalists get into the game to make money. We're there because we love it. It's why people say we have ink in our veins. In any event, she lost all credibility at that very moment. A day or two later, I think, I demanded complete control as a means to an end. I did not want her involved in any shape or form."

Carolyn refused to grant him control, while concurrently insisting that there was nothing *to* control. Things were going nowhere.

Late in the winter of 2008, with no conference host or plan for one, it looked like the Tenth Great would be cancelled. It was then, so the story goes, that a group of obit writers from Portland stepped forward to fill the convention void. The Society of Professional Obituary Writers formed quickly and tossed up a website. Their first conference, which focused on the obit-writing craft, was intended for obituary writers only. No fans. No Apron Ladies. It was the different beast that the Canadians wanted, without the express rancor toward Carolyn's gatherings. spow scheduled its conference for April in Portland, Oregon, and all the journalists who had been without a conference snapped up reservations for this new one.

However, it was at this point that Carolyn rallied and rescheduled the Tenth herself, at the usual time, June, and at an old, beloved location, Las Vegas, New Mexico, the site of her second conference, the one tied to the beloved memory of the blue-and-green hearse.

The scene was set, with predictable results, at least for Carolyn: a Tenth Great Conference with far fewer attendees. Between the journalists who sided with the Toronto writers, those who wanted to steer clear of the whole kerfuffle, and those who had just plain used up their vacation days on the spow conference, the gathering that had helped revive the death beat was reduced to a ghost of its former self.

And it was hurtful, a few people said, the way spow had announced its own conference online. Lexy Chubrich, the schoolteacher with ambitions of writing obits herself someday, tells me over Saturday's lunch, "The number of times that I was told [on the website that] I wasn't welcome, or, 'If you're not a member, don't come,' was excessive. It seemed to be a jab at Carolyn. Because Carolyn, of course, is not an obituary writer. And then I thought, 'Well, oh my gosh, maybe too many people like me started to come, and now Carolyn is getting pushed out because they don't want all the riffraff!'" Indeed, in the organization's infancy in 2008, SPOW's website only explicitly opened up membership and invitation to its conference to "journalists who make a living from or get paid to write/edit obits." This would change in the years that followed, with varying membership levels and privileges offered to working obit writers and others.

It's a sad side effect of success, this unintended pitting of professionals against the fans who arguably made them. The biggest names here at the Tenth, writers Jim Sheeler and Kay Powell, seem keenly aware of the new tension, and they talk at volume and length about how thankful they are for all that Carolyn has done, and how fantastic it is that everyone traveled all this way.

On Saturday afternoon, in the last hours of the last day, Jim Sheeler gives his keynote presentation, a reading from his book *Final Salute*, which is not about obituaries–not really–but about military deaths in Iraq. At the same time, it's a book distinguished by the craft of the journalistic obit writer, specifically, the unflinching detail and intimacy that has won Sheeler the Pulitzer. *Final Salute* is two-hundred-some pages of everyman obit. His depictions of army widows locked in grief are so poignant that he gets choked up a few times trying to read from his own work. At the break, I splash cold water on my face in the hotel's dimly lit ladies' room. I'm thinking about how well Jim's presentation encapsulates this conference's big-tent spirit, celebrating all the things an obit can be and all it can become. Then I wonder: Would I be feeling the same surge of charitable satisfaction had the closing speaker been a town elder, or the Apron Lady? It's doubtful.

I've spent these two days working out a theory in my head about the rival factions of obit writers and fans. There's this idea that the writers who attended the new SPOW conference instead of this one want to turn their backs on that spirit that birthed their success. The more I consider it, though, the more I think it's just what happens. The demise of the Great Obituary Conference existed in its very conception. For years, here was the sole opportunity for practitioners and fans of a narrow genre, underappreciated for so long, to convene and exalt it. That very act of veneration helped turn it into something else, something more. And the presence of all those odd hangers-on whom Carolyn loves only helped guarantee that someday the obituary would need a venue of its own, to showcase its maturity and singularity rather than its commonality with other forms of storytelling. It's a little like the obituary itself. In the first decade of the twenty-first century, the genre is experiencing an egalitarian phase. The everyday joes and the family pets are getting their moments in the sun, but maybe there will be a backlash against this, too, when cultural tides shift and we deem it time to restrict the number of guests at our collective memory's table.

As for Carolyn Gilbert, she's far from finished. Late Saturday afternoon, when the last glass water pitcher is long drained, she tells us she plans to schedule next year's Great conference on the opposite end of the calendar from the spow convention, which she amicably calls "a completely different group from ours, with a real difference in motive." She has a longer-term goal, too: to inaugurate a real physical place that celebrates the obituary all year long, a repository she calls the "obituarium." She laughs as she says the word, but may God strike you dead if you think she's kidding. She says that she has tried working with several universities on the project, but that each has wanted to take complete control of it, to accept her sizeable collections of news clips as donations. Unsurprisingly, Carolyn has not taken a shine to this approach. So she's still considering her options.

To hear her talking about it this way—with no real specifics, in the last, lazy minutes of the conference, several years after she and a few others came up with the notion one night over drinks at another Great—well, it all sounds kind of pie-in-the-sky. But then again, this is the woman who arranged the first-ever gathering of obituarists, something weird and unheard of ten years ago, on a dare. Who am I to call her crazy?

The Tenth Great Conference turned out to be the last Great Conference after all. The next year, Carolyn folded up operations, deciding that a gathering of a dozen people wasn't worth the time and money she routinely sank into the events. The Society for Professional Obituary Writers continued to meet for several years, but at the time of this writing, the organization that, in one sense, usurped the group that birthed it finds itself in a time of transition. The director, Alana Baranick, formerly an obit writer for the *Cleveland Plain Dealer* (and also coauthor of *Life on the Death Beat*, an insightful how-to on the craft of the obit writer), says she's ready to give up the reins to someone new. It's funny, she says. "One reason for reorganizing is that, try as I might to get other people to do things, it's been kind of a one-woman show here. And that was the very reason we started the organization—because the conference *you* went to was a one-woman show that was run by a woman who wasn't an obituary writer. We'd thought, 'We're going to do this more democratically.'"

But then Alana found herself in that position so familiar to people who run events: She ended up doing a lot of the work herself. And at this point in her life, in her sixties and semiretired, she's tired of it.

Besides, the obit world has changed.

Buyouts. Layoffs. Early retirements. In addition to Alana Baranick, here's an incomplete list of obit writers who, for reasons related to the newspaper's swift decline, are no longer living life on the death beat: Joan Harvey, formerly of the *Oregonian*; Jim Sheeler, formerly of the *Rocky Mountain News*; Kay Powell, formerly of the *Atlanta Journal-Constitution*; and Claire Martin of the *Denver Post*. (Other prominent obit writers have died or retired before the great newspaper decline: progenitors like Alden Whitman of the *New York Times* and Hugh Massingberd of the *Daily Telegraph*, who died in 1990 and 2007 respectfully. The *Washington Post*'s Richard Pearson died in

2003. And then there's the *Philadelphia Daily Inquirer*'s Jim Nicholson, who is not deceased as of this writing, only retired since 2001.)

A few stars remain: Stephen Miller at the *Wall Street Journal*, Adam Bernstein at the *Washington Post*, and Margalit Fox at the *New York Times*. And there are journalists at the Toronto's *Globe and Mail* and London's *Daily Telegraph* who continue to pen sprawling obituaries whose generous word-count allowances would make most American newspaper reporters green.

But those seasoned writers for midsized papers, the ones who wrote news obituaries about everyday joes—they're largely gone. The tables of *any* obit conference today would see a lot more empty chairs than those of yesteryear.

Some papers still cover the death beat. In many instances, however, the position has been tossed back, once again, to greener writers who collect smaller paychecks. When a paper has gotten rid of its best, most seasoned reporters—those with the deepest contacts and the strongest writing skills—the result, sometimes, is that the material just isn't as good. It's sentimental. Or superficial. Kay Powell says that too many obits these days take "the path of least resistance." She points to one the *Atlanta Journal-Constitution* ran in July 2012, when Don Perry, who led PR for the fast-food company Chick-Fil-A, died. His death took place in the middle of a public flap after company CEO Don Cathy made comments opposing gay marriage to a Christian publication. Cathy's statements drew attention to the company's large donations to antigay groups such as Focus on the Family and became a lightning rod for an explosive debate. The issue had long been simmering in the public imagination and now it boiled up, on late-night TV, daytime talk radio, barstools, kitchen tables, and social networking sites across the country. Chick-Fil-A locations everywhere became staging grounds, for "Support Chick-Fil-A" events sponsored by anti-gay-marriage groups and a "gay kiss" event staged by groups in favor. Several days into this fervor, Chick-Fil-A's chief spokesman Don Perry died of a heart attack. Whether or not the stress of the preceding days had somehow contributed to his death was a question being posed by amateur and professional pundits everywhere. The obit that came out on Monday, July 30, in the *Atlanta Journal-Constitution*, however, made no mention of the fracas. The feature consisted of several paragraphs about Perry's company loyalty, his Christian faith, his love for his family, and his genial personality—but there was not one word about the gay marriage controversy of the summer of 2012.

Kay Powell calls this poor journalism. "He is head of PR when the company is in the biggest PR mess it has ever faced. He dies—and not one mention? That, in my opinion, takes it out of the category of news obit, and into that of eulogy."

Not everyone agrees with Kay. She says she had lunch with one working reporter who thought that mentioning the scandal in his obit would have meant sensationalizing the death. And the reporter who actually wrote the piece pointed out to me that the paper had run another story in the paper's business section, which did mention the controversy. Beyond that, she said, her editor did not give her leave to comment.

To be fair, newspaper journalists today are a lot busier than they were when Kay sat at the desk. Besides interviewing, fact checking, and writing, reporters are often responsible for providing web versions and photography for their articles. That's not the least of it, said a different reporter, who left the paper around the same time as Kay. "In the old days, you had one story to do, you wrote it, you turned it in. Now, they've collapsed beats, so a writer is covering several different stories, and tweeting updates on them all day long." Or, there are just a lot fewer people covering a given beat, which has the same net effect. This is certainly the case at the *AJC*'s obit desk. When a reporter has a mountain of tasks on his daily agenda, choosing the path of least resistance in one of them might turn out to be the only realistic choice in order to survive the day and meet deadline.

Increasing online presence is just one strategy papers are employing to survive declining circulation and ad revenue. Another is scrapping news obits altogether in favor of paid, family-written obituaries. In recent years, a few papers have taken the further step of charging online readers special fees to read obits–which they still know to be a popular section. Veteran journalist and obit writer Jade Walker tells me, "The problem with obits now is that they're not a money-making venture for [papers]. People still love to read them, but [newspapers] aren't going to pay a reporter if they can get money from the families."

In a time when many print dailies are folding altogether, opportunities to make money can mean the difference between life and death for a paper. Hundreds now partner with paid site Legacy.com, which means that if you visit the obit page for the *Portland Press Herald* in Maine, the *Boonville Daily News* in Missouri, or even the *Pacific Daily News* in Guam, you'll see nearly identical webpages. Legacy provides a neatly organized, searchable site; with the click of a mouse, readers can learn about recent deaths and forthcoming funerals all over the country.

What's lost when the news obituary is replaced with a service that simply indexes family-written obits is a specific type of historical document. The news obituary is a specific genre of work. It's written by a trained professional who takes the time to learn the story of the deceased by talking with parents, ex-wives, and drinking buddies. A writer whose view is unclouded by the natural affections and prejudices that spring from longtime human relationships. Whose facts are straight and whose first goal is truth, flattering or ugly or complex as that truth may be. And while only one or two people in a given community may garner a news obit in a given day, those days add up. They form a record of a people, one that's rendered just a little less fascinating when most of its accounts come down to amateur obit clichés like, "She was beloved by all" and "He never met a stranger."

Of course, it's not a simple matter of arguing in favor of the historic and artistic merit of the news obituary. A whole lot of people working in print journalism appreciate the genre–in theory. At the same time, the revenue from paid obits may be what's allowing them to keep their own reporting jobs.

Nor is this the whole story. While this may be a tale about death, it's also a tale about rebirth, since we are cursed and blessed to live through these interesting times: to witness the demise of the newspaper and to see what's on the other side. As Jade Walker said to me near the end of a conversation about falling readership, about loss of advertising dollars and about layoffs in the newspaper industry, "You know, I don't want this to be a gloom-and-doom thing."

Walker, a veteran journalist who has written for the *Times* and currently writes for the *Huffington Post*, insisted on one point: It's an *exciting* time. Full of Sturm und Drang, yes, but also something else: opportunity. "We have so many options available to us in technology that we can really take things to the next level. I, for one, am excited."

She points out that obits are still the places people rush, in droves, when there's news of a celebrity death. The only difference between now and twenty years ago is that instead of dashing out to buy the next morning's paper, a death means people hurry to open up their laptops or iPads.

Recently, one of my writing heroes died. I combed Google, reading everything I could find: every remembrance, every obit, every posthumous profile. I listened to recordings of him reading his work. In one moment, hardly conscious of what I was doing, I even searched his image to see what he'd looked like in his thirties, when that first book came out; his forties, when he was in the prime of his success; and this decade, this year, when the cancer came back. The last days. In other words, I stalked him. Only the man was not alive. What fed my behavior was knowing he was truly out of reach now. There would be no more next book, no more next radio or magazine appearance. No more fresh ideas from that beautiful mind. The keen awareness of this absence made me–made many of us–fill our senses with all we appreciated about this writer before letting him go.

This sort of behavior, say journalists like Jade Walker, betrays a fascination that's largely underserved still. Online obituaries mean death-beat writers can link to primary-source material that readers are ravenous for whether the dead is a celebrity or not. Depending on the deceased's level of technological integration–*Did he blog? Is there video footage of her jazz ensemble on YouTube? Did he chat with an avid online quilting community?*–there might be quite a wealth of primary source material for the enterprising journalist. (Of course, social media pages themselves become memorials after someone dies. The online service *if I die* takes things a step further, allowing clients to film final web videos that the company delivers posthumously to Facebook friends. Says the cheeky British voice on the company's video ad, "Now, you're probably thinking to yourself, 'I don't remember scheduling an appointment with death anytime soon.' And you're right. And so is death: right–around the corner.")

"To actually have audio or footage or blogs of the people," says Jade Walker, "is priceless to an obituary writer [like me]. Because I didn't get the privilege of meeting them. So it lets me meet them just a little bit, and make my obit just that much more authentic."

The *New York Times* has begun filming a series of ultrashort documentaries called "The Last Word." These multimedia obits highlight interview footage taken in the final years of a subject's life. This footage is intended *for* this postdeath feature. Humorist Art Buchwald's 2007 piece begins with him looking straight into the camera and saying, "Hi! I'm Art Buchwald, and I just died." The Buchwald short also includes photo montages and B-roll of places like Buchwald's last home, all layered with thoughtful scoring and narration.

What features like these demonstrate is that even in a world potentially saturated with primary source material, a calculated narrative structure still provides meaning. Social media posts may tell the world about your sister's days of training and eventual finish time in that marathon. It may detail everything from her political concerns two summers ago to her Wednesday doldrums from some week last February. But even when added to her online photo stream and her comments on the local weekly's website, the sum total of all this content doesn't quite tell a story. A story has a structure, something a writer provides. A writer decides what to focus on and where to cut. Where the story begins, where it picks up momentum. And where it ends.

This may be the reason the obit isn't dead. The reason that Carolyn Gilbert, five years after the demise of her beloved conferences, soldiers on in her headstrong way through this uncertain light, same as she ever did. She never did create her obituarium—that physical repository of obit history—but she is conducting interviews with great obit writers and posting them online: Adam Bernstein and Kay Powell telling stories of the best obit they've ever written. The weirdest. The most touching. And me, I click, watch, and listen. Because I'm interested in stories about the dead.

CHAPTER FIVE

Give Me That Old-Time Green Burial

To get to Ramsey Creek Preserve, the first green-burial cemetery in the nation, you have to find your way to Westminster, South Carolina, a settlement tucked unobtrusively into the Appalachian foothills where the corners of North and South Carolina meet. And to find Westminster, you have to drive down a series of two-lane roads that dip and curve for signless miles through farmland and forest. The nearest interstate, I-85, doesn't even acknowledge the existence of Westminster; the online directions to Ramsey Creek are baffling. It's easier just to ask for directions from someone who lives somewhere along the way.

Better yet, follow Ramsey Creek cofounder Kimberley Campbell as she drives from town to the preserve. But you've got to pay attention to keep up as she takes those curves fast, turns off Long Creek Highway onto a smaller road that winds through the woods past a few

Family of Jacob Seawright Freeman at the grave of son Chalmus,
New Canaan Baptist Church cemetery, Dallas, Georgia, 1905.

RVS, and finally turns into a small gravel driveway flanked by sand-stone boulders.

When you're fascinated by something and you search yourself to fig-ure out why and the answer turns out to be that you're also slightly repelled by this same thing, I've found that it's best to just look the phenomenon in the face. I read about green burial in a major mag-azine, and the same article mentioned, as an aside, that there was a green-burial cemetery located in South Carolina—just a state away from where I was leading my fairly cash-strapped life. It could be an overnight trip. I mentioned it to some friends who lived in a univer-sity town near Westminster and they insisted on putting me up. Now there was no reason not to visit.

I'd loved visiting historic cemeteries—Victorian jungles like Al-legheny Cemetery in Pittsburgh and Oakland Cemetery in Atlanta—but the appeal of those places was primarily historic. Walking wind-ing paths surrounded by marble monuments, it's easy never to consider the reality of actual human bodies a-moldering below one's feet. Today's trend of green burial, meanwhile, is death at its most ba-sic: no vaults, metal caskets, or even wooden caskets with metal fix-tures. At most, the deceased is buried in a plain biodegradable pine box or a wicker basket. There is something good and right and un-selfish about the above facts. They also stir up my claustrophobia—a very Victorian fear of being buried alive—as well as the visceral chill that strikes whenever I think of that old childhood song: "The worms crawl in, the worms crawl out, the worms play pinochle on your snout." What scares me is not the idea of a wilderness peopled with the human dead; it's placing myself in the position of one of those dead. That absolute intimacy with the earth. In other words, it's not the population of dead people that frightens me; it's the earth itself.

Meanwhile, Ramsey Creek Preserve's website promises an abun-dance of unspoiled nature, a thirty-three-acre sanctuary teeming with forest and field and stream and wildlife, as well as death. Before coming here, I talked with the Campbells on the phone. This time of year, early spring, was a gorgeous time to come see the place, they said. During this first conversation, Ramsey Creek's founder, Billy Campbell, seemed mostly interested in talking about which flowers would be blooming when I arrived rather than the number of bodies they'd be burying.

First things first. A "green" burial means interment without embalming fluids or anything else that isn't biodegradable. Burial without embalming is a longstanding tradition in Jewish customs, and almost no matter your religious tradition, it's likely that your great-great-grandparents buried their loved ones in a similar way.

Despite these cultural and historical ties, Billy Campbell's wife Kimberley, who oversees the preserve's day-to-day operations, says that Ramsey Creek raised the eyebrows of a number of its neighbors when it opened in 1996. "I mean, 'Are they throwing bodies in the woods?'" she intones with put-on foreboding as we stroll through the gravel parking lot. "There was some of that." Kimberley Campbell is petite and fit and redheaded. She is also jocular and British and likes to poke gentle fun at the traditional American way of death with its big caskets and fake flower wreaths. (I don't know what it is with this journey and its repeated run-ins with lively British women. I would someday like to have them all together for a noisy dinner party.)

Billy Campbell, on the other hand, grew up in Westminster. He is also the town physician. A patient of Dr. Campbell's once jokingly compared him to the proverbial vet who's also a taxidermist, whose sign reads, EITHER WAY, YOU GET YOUR DOG BACK.

The website was right—Ramsey Creek is quite tranquil. Walking a softly rutted path through a small meadow, I'm already won over. Tall grasses rustle, pines sway, and cardinals and wrens twitter and chirp.

It's peaceful as a graveyard, only more so.

Ministers used to leading families across tidy, manicured cemetery lawns sometimes hesitate at the dirt paths that curve down and around the forested hills here. "But a kind of change comes over them," says Kimberley. "I mean, the comments usually are, 'This is so peaceful. This is so calming. It just seems right. It just makes sense.'"

Most cemeteries today lack the grandeur of old graveyards. They resemble, instead, golf courses. They are often located in commercial districts. They share blocks with Taco Bells. Here in the South, many little country churches are gone, replaced by massive, vinyl-sided megachurches.

And the little church graveyards are being replaced by nothing.

Michael St. Pierre, former president of the National Funeral Directors' Association, says that as the old churches die, their parochial cemeteries are abandoned, and modern developments often just build right over the church burial grounds. The graves themselves find new homes in modern cemeteries, but the old graveyards are vanishing. "The biggest cost in operating the cemetery is the perpetual maintenance," says Pierre. "It's darned if you do, darned if you don't." It seems the issue of perpetual maintenance—we are dead a very long time—becomes critical sooner or later at just about any cemetery, whether a modern-day memorial park or the back acreage of some farmland that has been in the family for ages. With time, all burial land becomes historic.

For some cemetery owners, selling off portions of their land to real estate developers is a lucrative option. Meanwhile, the fastest-growing trend in the funeral industry is cremation, predicted by the Cremation Association of North America to outpace conventional burial by 2017. Most of the ashes produced each year end up not in cemeteries or memorial parks, but scattered across some landscape meaningful to the family, or enclosed in urns or boxes at the back of hall closets from Maine to Alaska. Cemetery operators are making a big push for columbariums, those stand-alone buildings that shelve between several dozen and several hundred urns.

Here at Ramsey Creek, there are no columbariums or monuments of any kind to mark the graves of the dead. There aren't even any vertical gravestones. Burial spots are marked instead by flat rocks from the creek. In about a hundred years, the names of the deceased won't be visible on these rocks at all. Other graves are unmarked altogether. The difference doesn't stop above ground, either. Green-burial cemeteries also tend to be far less densely populated than conventional cemeteries. The preserve can accept about forty-four burials for every acre. (At press time, about three hundred people are buried in Ramsey Creek's expanded seventy-four acres.) Conventional cemeteries, meanwhile, can average some thousand burials per acre.

The fact is, graves are actually not the chief concern here. Conservation is. The Campbells reserve the right to move someone's intended burial site, for example, if that spot turns out to be home to a sensitive colony of plants. When they dig up the soil, they set aside the plant-containing layer to be replaced once the grave has been covered over. You can't tell the place is a cemetery right away because many of the graves have just disappeared into the woods.

This isn't true for every grave, however. As grassy meadow turns to forest and the gravel walkway becomes a dirt path, shafts of light break through the trees here and there, and Kimberley begins pointing out the little hollows she and Billy have dug out beneath the flat stones. The hollows are dwelling places for ants. She tells me ants are responsible for distributing between 80 and 90 percent of all wildflower seeds. The lesson puts me in the mood of summer camp. She points to a lumpy spot to the left of the dirt trail and says that it could be confused for a pit-mound disturbance, which is a spot where a tree has been uprooted, resulting in an upheaval of soil and an explosion of new organic activity, a common occurrence in forestland like this.

"As you can see with the graves," she says, breezily pointing to the spot, "we dig them about three feet deep. But then we don't take any of the soil away. It all goes back." Which means you end up with a mound about three feet high, and, for a while at least, the body rests at about six feet under. In about two years' time, the body decomposes and the dirt settles again.

She does call it a body, by the way—not an "expired individual" or a "person who's passed." When Billy Campbell talks about shoveling dirt onto a casket, he doesn't call it "closing the gravesite," he calls it a "burial." This doesn't seem unusual until you start talking with conventional funeral-home types, for whom digging a grave becomes "opening an interment space," who refer to ashes as "cremains" and someone's mother who has just died as "the decedent" (a term adopted from the legal world).

An entire idiom has been created with the aim of shielding a grief-stricken clientele, a palliative language meant to create a distance between the living and the experience of death. At Ramsey Creek, that language is absent because the distance is, too. In its place, the Campbells apply a gentle frankness that appeals to their self-selecting clientele.

On our walk, Kimberley takes a couple of cell phone calls from prospective customers. She talks one person through her options: Go with a funeral home for a service before burying the body here, or simply use the funeral home for storage until the family is ready for a service at Ramsey Creek. She also gives some pointers on holding a service at home. "Lots of dry ice," she says. It's the torso you need to concentrate on, since that's the space that holds the organs, which break down quickly. At one point, after a good long listen, Kimberley says, "Well, you know, the funeral directors have a license to embalm. That's basically what their license is for. And, you know, that's it."

I checked this. In South Carolina law, funeral directors receive funeral service licenses. "Practice of funeral service" means:

1. providing shelter, care, and custody of the human dead;
2. preparing the human dead by embalming or other methods for burial or other disposition;
3. arranging for the transportation of the human dead;
4. making arrangements to provide any of the above services, or selling funeral merchandise.

So, to enlarge Kimberley's above statement: People who don't hold funeral licenses in South Carolina can't transport, shelter, or embalm bodies. That's the way it is in most states. If you're not a funeral director, you can't proffer or perform services related to the disposition of bodies, the centerpiece of which is, yes, embalming, the specialized skill at the heart of funeral direction. Holding a license also tends to entail a great deal of responsibility regarding multitudes of state regulations that funeral pros must follow. This system of regulation is reassuring to a lot of people. But home-funeral and green-burial proponents think it's problematic to have an entire set of legalities in place where there once were few. This set of laws that change from state to state do nothing but further distance us from our dead, they say, just like embalming, the practice at the center of it all.

Of course, it wasn't always this way. Until the advent of the twentieth century in urban areas, and even later in rural areas and many parts of the South, families held funerals at home in the United States. At that time, an undertaker would use your family's kitchen to clean, dress, and prepare bodies for viewing and service. The kitchen provided ready access to water and usually a back door, and like the funeral home basements that came after, it could also be counted upon to be uncarpeted–which made it far easier to clean up any messy bodily fluids if embalming had taken place.

This was also the era of the cooling board–that once-ubiquitous piece of furniture that I saw six or seven of in the pitch-perfect displays at the Museum of Funeral Customs. The sight of an object on a museum shelf calcifies its place in the temporal continuum: History. Obscurity. The idea of carrying those cooling boards across the velvet museum rope to use again is wholly strange, as is the idea of making new ones. However, in all but a few states, it's actually not against the law to hold funeral services at home. This is a fact that today's green-burial and home-funeral proponents love to point out. And it's just one misconception about what's true–and what isn't–when it comes to rules today for tending to the dead.

Another fallacy is that if a body is not cremated, it is required by law to be embalmed. (It's not, in any of the fifty states.) Yet another is that burial vaults–those big cement boxes that caskets are buried inside of–are also required by law. Vaults were invented in the 1800s to prevent resurrectionists–a.k.a. grave robbers–from stealing bodies to sell to medical labs and universities for study. Today, most vaults are marketed according to their relative merits in terms of body preservation. But the reason conventional cemeteries require them is so that the ground covering the grave doesn't sink in the weeks and months following the burial.

Most of the misconceptions regarding death and burial laws revolve around the idea that a dead body becomes something contagious rather quickly, that it becomes dangerous to handle. Kimberley Campbell says drily, "That is just not the truth. We're far more contagious alive. Dead men don't sneeze."

It's an understandable fear, she says, bred by unfamiliarity and the horror of death. People wonder if they can really hold a home funeral, not just whether it's legal, but whether a casket in the living room is something they could handle emotionally; they want to know how soon the body begins to stink, how soon the skin changes, how soon the person we love stops being the person we love–and becomes something else.

This concern has helped the funeral business grow into a twenty-billion-dollar-a-year industry, one that profits mostly from a host of expenses that have nothing to do with a hole in the ground. A typical funeral business earns most of its living from casket sales. According to a recent survey from the NFDA, most Americans end up paying around $2,200 for a metal casket. Wooden caskets are more expensive–around $2,800. A bronze model with fourteen-karat-gold-plated hardware and velvet interior goes for more than $20,000, while cremation caskets purchased at funeral homes run between $895 and a little over $1,000. You can purchase the vaults that most conventional cemeteries require for anywhere from $975 to $16,000. And then there's transportation: At a successful funeral home in Wilmington, North Carolina, operated by one of the biggest funeral chains in the country, hearses for the deceased cost $250, optional limos for the living run $320 each, and the flower truck runs $120. There's the basic service fee for the time of the funeral director and staff ($3,495). Embalming, dressing, "casketing," and refrigeration of the body ($995 + $295 + $295). Also: rental of the little machine that lowers the casket into the ground, the funeral register book, and that piece of bright green Astroturf that surrounds the grave on the day of the funeral. At the successful North Carolina business, funeral packages run between $11,000 and $24,000. The fastest-growing funeral practice, a memorial service plus cremation, runs between $6,000 and $12,000. For some people experiencing death, every one of these costly elements becomes a necessity.

Others view it differently. Especially non-Americans. For one perspective, I turned to Christine Parker, a conventional funeral director in Great Britain who used to lead that country's Society of Allied and Independent Funeral Directors. It turns out that the noisy reputation of the United States does not stop at the grave. These were not her words. What she did say, gently and politely, was that most prospective clients in her country are turned off by the showy pomp associated with American funerals. "I have clients who will ask me," she says, "if we are 'connected to that American lot,'" meaning companies like Service Corporation International, whose funeral homes are often run under the name Dignity Memorial.

   SCI spent the 1980s buying up funeral homes all over the United States and Great Britain. Its promotion of the comparably elaborate, expensive American way of death left a bad taste in the mouths of many Britons, who she says are reluctant "to have anything other than a traditional British funeral." That's a closed-casket service followed by cremation, rather than the embalming, the hearses, and all of the trimmings listed above. About 74 percent of Britons choose cremation, compared to 40 percent of Americans. Meanwhile, many Americans who choose cremation choose direct cremation, without a service involving the body, and often zero interaction with it either.

The whole death experience at Ramsey Creek—including grave digging, optional casket (purchased or built elsewhere), and service—

runs, on average, about $4,000. A burial plot costs $2,500–which is actually more expensive than the cost of most graves at conventional cemeteries. Most states, South Carolina included, require that 10 to 15 percent of the price for any burial plot go toward a long-term trust to maintain the property as cemetery land. At Ramsey Creek, where the ultimate goal is land preservation, more money per grave goes toward that fund.

Billy Campbell, whose lifelong passion outside of medicine is botany and conservation, has worked to restore the natural character of Ramsey Creek's thirty-four wooded acres. His pie-in-the-sky dream is to eventually help save a million acres of natural land through green burial.

For services like storing and transporting the body, the Campbells refer families to conventional funeral homes. For cards and books, there's the big-box bookstore over in Greenville about an hour away. As for the Astroturf, there isn't any. The little machine that lowers the casket is absent, too. Billy, Kimberley, and a team of assistants dig the graves. Family members are welcome to help, and at many services they lower the pine box or enshrouded body into the ground themselves.

"As it happens, as they work," says Billy, "the men who haven't said anything at all, they'll start telling stories about the person they're helping to cover up, in a way they wouldn't have otherwise. But they're out there working, and somehow it's a little easier to do, when you've been out there exerting yourself for a while. There is something about that experience, I think, that most people find oddly comforting."

If you want to get under Billy Campbell's skin quickly, call him a New Ager. It's a label he says they heard a lot from the local media and from folks in the conventional funeral industry when he and Kimberley opened Ramsey Creek fourteen years ago. Billy Campbell was particularly incensed by a web comment that lumped Ramsey Creek in with a trend of "liberal, PC funerals."

"I mean, what part of Genesis 3:19 do you find to be so liberal and radical? 'For dust you are, and to dust you will return.' Pumping the body full of chemicals and looking like you're alive in your best suit, that's more like a pseudo-Egyptian, new-agey kind of thing to me." Billy Campbell is not a crystal-toting, astrology-reading kind of guy. The fifty-seven-year-old physician was raised in Westminster as a strict Southern Baptist. He's lanky, with a face best described as open: a big, ready smile that reveals big, white teeth, and ears that are proportional to all of it. Generous.

"It was all God's creation, growing up," he says. He was born again at fourteen, and a few years later fell away from the literal aspects of that belief, from what he calls "the fairytale stories." Still, it's with an unmistakable missionary zeal that he talks about man's responsibility to the earth. "If you have a truth, then you need to share it." He spends his lunch breaks walking the grounds of Ramsey Creek, noting the minute changes he sees from day to day and season to season. Most of our conversations return to these changes: The pink lady's slipper is flowering; the persimmons are ripe; he's found an explosion of pine beetles today.

Billy spent his childhood running around the same old-growth forest where he and Kimberley now live. His childhood entomological and botanical projects (read: boxes and jars of bugs and plants) gave way, once he grew up, to endeavors like purchasing land for preservation in Costa Rica and North Carolina. He also founded South Carolina Forest Watch, which monitors timber harvesting in the state.

But the trigger that inspired this work was the death of his father in the early 1990s. Billy realized that with the equivalent of what it cost for the funeral, he could have bought ten acres of land as a permanent memorial to his father. In 1996 Billy founded Memorial Ecosystems, Ramsey Creek's parent company. Now he's considered a pioneer of the green-burial movement to people like Joe Sehee, who directs the Green Burial Council, an organization that has established standards and oversight for green-burial cemeteries. Sehee says that attempts at green burial in Great Britain in the early 1990s lacked much of a scientific approach (at many sites, folks would just plant a tree atop a grave and call it green). With his rigorous knowledge of botany and ecology, Billy has introduced the complex and often delicate matter of ecosystem preservation to the process. In other words, he has made the land's needs as much a priority as the needs of the person who wants to be buried with only a shroud.

Joe Sehee says that acceptance of green burial by the mainstream funeral industry has been slow in coming. He compares it to the fabled resistance to cremation in the 1970s and '80s. "For far too long," he says, "they argued with the market instead of listening to it." It's hardly a surprise that funeral directors dug in their heels; as a method of disposition, cremation has increasingly eaten away at the industry's major forms of income—sales of fancy vaults, caskets, and embalming. A few decades later, on a smaller scale, green burial does the same, leaving traditional funeral service providers a similar tricky line to walk, between safeguarding their livelihoods and giving customers what they want.

Apart from the 296 people buried at Ramsey Creek Preserve, 200 more are in the process of purchasing plots. Most of them are babyboomers—no surprise when you consider that this generation spearheaded trends like home birthing, hospice, and getting married on the beach.

But there are also people in their eighties and nineties buried here, Depression babies attracted by the comparatively modest prices associated with green burial and the memory of funerals they attended long ago. In the midst of waxing rhapsodic about sustainable development and conserving land, Kimberley pauses. "I mean, I hate to say it's a win-win option, because somebody obviously has to die."

One woman I spoke with, Elizabeth Stuckman, has a brother, Stuart, buried at Ramsey Creek. At the funeral, a friend identified the sourwood tree beside the burial site as the subject of one of Stuart's favorite bluegrass songs. Now she refers to her visits to Ramsey Creek as "visiting Stuart's tree." She says, "Now, I don't think of him in that hole. I look at the tree and at the treetops and think, 'Stuart is there. He is all around.'" Most of us seek something larger out of death–some promise of an afterlife, some assurance of permanence just when that permanence feels most threatened. At Ramsey Creek, assurance is found in a patch of impatiens growing where a son lies, or in the mountain laurel that blooms above a mother's grave, or in the sourwood rooted where a brother is buried. In this way, the dead literally become part of the living. Some say that's as close to heaven on earth as you can get.

Oana Hogrefe,
Memorial Photographer

Memory Maker

Oana Hogrefe had just returned to her day job after forty-eight exhausting hours coaching a woman through childbirth. It was Oana's first experience working as a doula–an intensive, nonmedical birthing assistant. While training, she had learned about a group of volunteer photographers in Atlanta who take infant "remembrance" photos for parents in the opposite situation: those sad cases when newborns have died or have been given terminal diagnoses. The invitation stirred something in her, a sense of intrigue and duty. Without hesitation, she put her name on the interest sheet that was going around the room. Weeks passed, then months.

And it was this day, after her first experience helping a mother bring a child into the world, that she got her first call from a hospital about a death. A new mother wanted a set of remembrance photographs of her dying newborn.

Oana is no timid soul. She'd photographed the dead before, had always felt drawn, in fact, to documenting birth and death, what she calls "transitions, those crucial times in our lives." Still, this call was jarring, coming now, when her eyelids felt like sandpaper every time she closed them—and when she did, fervent images from the last forty-eight hours came flooding back. She had also just missed two days at her regular job as a software developer. Her lunch break, which she had planned on working through, was just about to start. By any common-sense judgment, she could take a pass this once.

Instead, she found herself thinking of providence, and she found herself saying "Yes" to the nurse on the phone. At the hospital, she walked into a room where a girl young enough to be her own daughter sat on a bed under fluorescent lights, crying, beside a newborn who had died already. In her subsequent experience, cases like this are rare; usually, Oana arrives before an infant is taken off life-support machinery. But this baby had died of causes unknown just after his birth. The teenager mother's real mother was absent. "I hugged her," says Oana, "and I told her that I was proud of her."

Oana is in her late thirties, although there's a pixie-like ageless-ness about her face; at a rare trip to a bar recently, she was carded by a concerned bartender who took her for a twenty-year-old. That day at the hospital, she says, "All I knew is I couldn't rush this girl." She took a full two hours there, snapping photographs. The teenager wanted to hold the child, wanted to have lots of physical contact before letting go, and this, Oana says, was good. She took dozens of pictures, to give the girl something she couldn't create on her own after this loss: a specific kind of memory. One that was beautiful.

In her photos, the subjects—mother, sometimes father, and infant—are all we ever see. A baby lies on a soft expanse of white sheet, grasping an adult finger—the father's—in its tiny hand. In another, the mother cradles the infant close. Her expression varies from still to still: vulnerable and breaking in one, all maternal confidence in the next; and in another, she's sunk down deep inside herself, inscrutable. And so on. The backgrounds are muted and blurred. We don't seem to be in a hospital. The landscapes are instead composed completely of humanity. There are no elements foreign to the private experience of mother, father, and baby, and each is so candid, it's hard to believe Oana herself is there.

Oana has photographed more than a dozen dying and deceased infants since she started volunteering two years ago. Whenever she is called for an assignment, there are certain things she needs to know. When the nurse, chaplain, or social worker phones, she'll find out the cause of death if it is known and the age of the infant. "Just to have a mental image of what it might look like. You know, because if it's a twenty-four, twenty-five-week-old little preemie, then it's much more challenging than somebody who was three months old and born at term. And I'm trying to prepare myself for the lighting," she says, although she brings only minimal gear. Also, she asks, will the parents be alone with the infant, or will others be present too—relatives or siblings? In some cases, an extended family packs a room, but her focus is always on the mother and father, who labor under the heaviest burden.

Early in our first conversation—over coffee, outside a strip mall on a crisp, bright morning—I ask her if that first call made her nervous. "Yeah!" Oana responds, in a way that sounds very close to, "Duhhhh!" and then she laughs. "I was trying to call everybody I knew, and random people! And telling them, 'I'm going to do this!'"

Today, we are talking about many horrible things. We are talking about infants who die in utero whose mothers have to go through labor anyway; young babies with genetic disorders whose parents live under an agonizing countdown to a day when they will decide to turn off the oxygen; Oana's own countdown three years ago as she watched her father deteriorate from Alzheimer's. When she brings up sensitive points about these difficult things, Oana laughs. It's not an inconsiderate laugh, and it's not uncomfortable. The first time it erupts, it feels neither surprising nor out of place. Instead, I feel like joining in. Oana's musical accent—she left Romania for the States fourteen years

ago–adds to the overall effect. Often, she talks through her laughter; the resultant vocal sound is sort of musical and could almost be
mistaken for crying to a person just walking by. Oana laughs when
relating something awful or funny or cringingly awkward or moving.
Somehow, her laugh signifies the intersection of all these emotions,
especially moments in which they become tangled beyond hope of
classification. It signifies, simply, feeling.

She gets nervous almost every time she steps through a hospital's
double doors with her camera gear. It's not that she's apprehensive
about the fairly predictable technical aspects of her role. The unique
challenge, every time, is the spectrum of raw emotion she knows she
will find in the parents. In cases when an infant was born with genetic disorders, he is likely to have been attached to life support for
months. His parents have had time–terrible days and weeks–to ad-
just to the idea of his probable death. If, however, a son or daughter
who was just born dies quickly, parents tend to be mired in shock and
a sense of unreality. This makes it harder for Oana to do her job with
the results she knows they want.

She tries, subtly, to counter this. Once in the hospital room, "I'm
being very quiet, I'm doing lots of eye contact. I'm commenting on
how beautiful the baby is; you know, there's always something beautiful about them, really. They have pretty fingers or something." By
pointing out such small truths and then documenting them on film,
she is trying to substantiate, gently, their real presence together in
the world.

"I just want to give them that space in which they are with the
child. So the more I see them getting into it and touching the child . . .
Sometimes I try to prompt that a little bit. You know, just say, 'Hold
his finger,' or something that makes it more skin-to-skin, just so they
have some body memory of having touched the child. Because to me,
that's part of their grieving."

The memory helps make the moment real, a concrete experience
of a brief life lived and a death and grief that cannot be denied, even

if the person who died was only a few hours old–or never lived outside his mother's womb at all. The experience is made even more significant by the fact that Oana has come as a volunteer on her lunch
break, or during her free evening hours rather than spending them
with her own children. To Oana, all these facts tell the parents that
theirs is a real tragedy, of real importance in the world. "You need to
acknowledge that for the mom–rather than say, 'Well, you have your
other children,' or, 'It was only a few months old.' That's not what you
want to hear. You want to hear, 'It was a horrible thing. It happened.
I'm sorry.'"

There is discomfort, sometimes, in her desire to make her job–arriv-
ing, taking photos, and leaving–truly meaningful. The moment she
gets called in, after all, is often the moment just before an infant is
to be disconnected from life-prolonging machines. The association
makes her feel like a Grim Reaper figure at times. "You know, 'Okay,
the photographer's here; let's disconnect the child!'" She laughs; the
association is *so* terrible. "That alone is spooky to me, so I never try
to speed up the process. You know, I'm just there."
    She will arrive and stay for one hour or three. She takes close-ups
of the baby's hands and feet. In her regular photography business, in
which she takes pictures of healthy children, Oana's trademark style
is natural and unposed, "but these parents here don't want a photo-
journalistic memory of what's going on. They want it a bit more idealized. Most people would like to envision the child how he could have
looked." So she works to create this memory. She focuses in close,
asks the mother if she wants to touch the face or arm. The baby, having been taken off an oxygen machine ten minutes before, may or may
not still be living. It's the toughest moment. "And it's not always easy
to tell. Some of them can breathe on their own for a little bit. Others
just sort of quickly expire."
    Behind the camera, Oana keeps her professional wits about her,
keeping track of what she's done and gauging what the family may
still want, but she's also experiencing these moments emotionally.

After the child is disconnected, the hospital chaplain will usually baptize him. "We all hold hands together, we pray, and I just become part of it–and that's when I start crying, usually. That's when it becomes the most difficult." She pauses. "And I try to document that time, too. To have a couple pictures of the water being dripped, or something being read, or whatever's going on." She does not try to establish any sort of professional distance, she says. It's more like she experiences a sort of split personality: there's her picture-taking self, and there's her personal self, who's witnessing this event. Once, after a session, she walked to the elevator and broke down in tears. At the next floor, the elevator stopped, and the dying baby's father got on. "And he was like, 'What's this for? Are you okay?'" She shakes her head, laughing. "I mean, *bawling*." Such cases are rare, though, and ultimately, the loss is not hers. "I'm not gonna own it for them."

Documenting an infant's death is the sort of hard work one could pretty much do only on a volunteer basis; its rewards are so intangible. Or, looked at another way, its rewards are so profound–validating a life the wider world might view as fairly insignificant and its sharp departure–that attaching an extrinsic price might do nothing but damage the poetry of its workings.

It was Oana's promise to the fates that led her to it. She has two healthy children. Her second child's birth was a successful vaginal delivery after a caesarian section with her first child–a risky medical endeavor. Late in her second pregnancy, she had promised herself, the fates, the universe, that if her girl was born healthy, she would become a doula and help other women through the same process. The memorial photography was just another side of the same coin, one that she felt she couldn't ignore, because in her own life such tragedy had, so far, ignored her.

She doesn't give grieving mothers anything tangible; she can't. What she does try to give is a sense of order at least, a particular kind of memory. A few months ago, a Hispanic woman gave premature birth to a set of triplets, two boys and a girl. The girls, though tiny and lying side by side in the NICU, were perfectly healthy. However, the boy, named Dario, had caught an infection and was sent to a separate hospital across the street for specialized treatment, where he died. "And the parents wanted me to take pictures of Dario, and then they asked: Could I go across the street and take pictures of his sisters, at that same moment?" Even though the triplets were in separate places, Oana's photography could create a tangible timeline, a full scene that they could translate later: They could place the picture of Dario at 3:17 p.m. right next to the picture of his sisters taken a few minutes before. In an uncontrollable world, this was the closest thing possible to order and sense. Many of Oana's photos attempt such a task. In this way, her work has a lot in common with that of an earlier generation of memorial picture takers. The first remembrance photos, taken in the nineteenth century by traveling photographers, would sometimes be the only pictures survivors had of the deceased. Often, entire families would pose with the dead, the resulting scene becoming proof of a sort: a set of familial bonds stamped by light onto paper, even in the shadow of mortality.

Today, thanks to modern medicine, people don't die too often from unknown causes. However, a gap remains in the realm of diagnosis of the youngest infants, whose causes of death sometimes baffle us, their small exits from this world shattering our belief in medicine's ability to protect us.

In the scenes she documents and often gently urges along, Oana creates a slightly stylized tableau, which is not to say that it's a false one. It creates a concrete set of events that parents can check back on later in their lives and see: their hands against his cheek, his head against her chest, alive for this minute, this one–and then not.

In a world in which we can control only so many circumstances surrounding an unborn infant's health, a lot of the burden ends up, inevitably, in the lap of the expectant mother. Her diet, her sleep patterns, her vitamin intake and consumption of classical music suddenly become the focus of a lot of attention. Mothers whose infants don't make it, says Oana, can't help but wonder where they went wrong. "You know: 'Why did you go into labor at twenty-four weeks? Was it something you ate? Was it something you didn't eat?' There's a lot of questioning in the parents' minds, especially if there's not a very clear diagnosis for why the child has died. If it's just, 'It happened.'" In the photos, there is an almost ritualistic restoration. The mothers and fathers are pictured, for the ages, as gentle caregivers. When they need to look back, the truth of that memory is right there, authenticated in beautiful, stark black and white.

In Oana's last memory of her father, his right hand is receding into the darkness of a crematory furnace. This was in Romania, where he died three years ago. "Such a strange thing," she says. "It was an open casket and they lowered him in, and then he got cremated. But this lowering is such a strange process–" she laughs as she speaks, even as her voice quavers, "you know, because you see him, and then he just disappears." Her father, who had Alzheimer's, had been leaving everyone by degrees for years, but his final leave-taking is not just a memory in Oana's mind's eye; she possesses photographic images of the ordeal. She snapped pictures of him in his decline, in his death ("He was beautiful, but very changed"), and in the moments his familiar figure retreated down into the shadows before the flames hit. "It's very weird," she says. That laugh again. "I wanted to own his life as much as I could. I was trying to touch him one more time and remember"–she pauses, hands reaching up and cradling the empty air between–"the shape of this."

Some people take home movies of watershed moments like births and funerals. Others find such documentation distasteful, simultaneously invasive and exhibitionistic. I'll admit that before talking to Oana, I lived in the latter camp. When I read about her work, my reaction was similar to my knee-jerk response to those old Victorian memorial photos. There was something grotesque in it. At least the Victorian photos had the distancing factor of time and culture shifts; the long intervening years made me less likely to look at those old photos and think of actual death or consider the subjects as actual people who had lived in this world in the same ordinary way I do. I could even relegate them to kitsch. But the purpose of Oana's work is the opposite of distancing. It's about contact: the parents' with their babies' fleeting lives and with the experience of their death, as well as their subsequent contact with that memory. If a woman wanted her to, Oana says she would volunteer to photograph the birth of a stillborn. She photographed her father in his death for the same reason, the way someone else might go home and compose a piano piece about it. To process the experience, to probe it and to suss out its complexities. To examine the greatest unknowns in the only way we can: by throwing ourselves into the evidence we can see, hear, and touch. The same way I'm writing about it right now.

Many of the photos she takes of parents holding their children capture the only time this happened. It is only by unhooking the tubes and wires keeping the infants alive that parents can finally cradle their children, and Oana is there to make that fleeting memory of closeness the one that persists. Earlier this year, she photographed a set of identical twin sisters, one of whom would die within days. When Oana arrived, the healthy twin was crying inconsolably until they laid her next to her sick sister, at which point she calmed at once and fell asleep, and Oana leaned in at once and began photographing. "And they were beautiful, very sweet photos." She often tries to get older siblings, if they're around, into the pictures. Later in life, she says, the surviving sibling, the living man or woman, can find this old picture, can look at it, and see: "'Here we are, close together.' At least that makes it real."

REVEALED:

How morticians became funeral directors,
and Don Wilkerson's
Life in Death

CHAPTER SIX

The House Where Death Lives

In the waning days of the nineteenth century, the funeral home was a brand-new American business, as novel as the motion-picture camera, cotton candy, and the steel-framed skyscraper and as eager to establish itself to an inquisitive public. The undertaker had been around for a while, but the funeral director—who knew how to embalm and who took care of all the concerns one associated with funerals under one roof—was new. Pages from town directories from at least as early as the 1700s list the profession "Layer Out of Bodies." It was a job often held by women who also worked as midwives. Until the very end of the 1800s, and even later in rural areas and much of the South, no one person took care of all the roles we associate with a funeral director. Instead, the operation was carried out piecemeal. Under the orders of physicians making home calls, families would first oversee the business of dying itself, from bleeding the sick to closing the eyes of the dead and tying the jaw shut with muslin.

Horses and carriages in front of the funeral home of
C. W. Franklin, undertaker, Chattanooga, Tennessee, 1899?

(Interestingly, bloodletting remained popular in the United States through the 1800s. Virginia Terpening, director of the Indiana Medical History Museum, tells me, "There was this idea that you could have too much blood, and that there might actually be bad blood. Problem was, they thought the body had a great deal more blood than there actually was." As the practice declined, debate raged between those Civil War physicians who believed in bloodletting's efficacy and those who did not. Phlebotomy is recommended as late as 1920 in at least one American medical text, which dictates that "To bleed at the very onset in robust, healthy individuals in whom disease sets in with great intensity and high fever is good practice."[1])

When someone in your household died, you might call upon your local carpenter. He made tables and shelves, so naturally he made coffins and put people in them, too. Or else he made a living selling or renting out carriages and horses, a universal occasion for such being, of course, the transport of the dead to graveyards.

By the late 1800s, however, a transition began to take hold. "If we know any good thing," brags an announcement in *The Casket* magazine for the first annual meeting of the Funeral Directors of Michigan, "let us let our Brothers have the benefit of it and we will only feel better for it. The people at large expect more of us now than they did a few years ago. All they wanted of an undertaker then was to make or furnish them a coffin and they would have some friend or neighbor take charge of the funeral; but now it is far different. As soon as their dear one passes away they send for the Funeral Director, and they say to him, 'We want you to take full charge and do what you think best.'"[2]

The display on one wall at the Museum of Funeral Customs is laugh-out-loud alarming. "The Long Motor pays him. It will pay you!" shouts the 1915 ad from *Embalmers Weekly*, in which a well-dressed, rather smug-looking man stands beside his hearse–which he also uses as a town ambulance. This particular duality of purpose went on in some places until the late 1970s, it turns out–around the time my mother had to call an ambulance when she was in labor with me. Finally, there's an amateur photo here from around 1940 that pictures the long side of a black hearse with its door swung open. Inside, a young, white-capped nurse, her face a mask of efficiency, sits beside a reclining old woman who looks gray faced and disoriented. You want to make a joke about it, but it feels uncomfortable: Their port of call is not clear.

Today's typical funeral business is a family business. It's a profession built on trust, which is often based on reputations that run generations deep. In terms of square inches on glossy pamphlets and websites, the amount of marketing space that funeral homes dedicate to broadcasting their own integrity is considerable. This makes sense. When your father dies, the character of the people handling his physical remains and his memory matters to you. It also makes sense considering the storm of attack brought on by the publication in 1963 of Jessica Mitford's book *The American Way of Death*. The work criticized the commercialized nature of the funeral trade; it also exposed financial deceit by businesses across the country. Funeral pros have spent the five decades since countering the public's lingering distrust.

Actually, they've spent longer than that. Perhaps more than any other trade, funeral direction is built on a solid history of constantly reassuring the public. Take the new funeral directors at the turn of the twentieth century, whose job it was to convince the public for the first time that they were the ideal one-stop shop for getting the casket, calling the preacher, and getting the flowers, too.

Stephen George Wilkerson was among these enterprising young upstarts. A well-known county coroner, Stephen George saw the possibility of major success in the new business of death. It was 1932, and like many rural and southern places across the nation, his town of Greenville, North Carolina, was only just starting to move away from the tradition of the home funeral. Greenville was a small town–the population in 1930 was just under ninety-two hundred–but it was growing year by year into the square miles of cotton fields surrounding it. Upon establishing S. G. Wilkerson and Sons, Stephen George faced a diverse set of unprecedented challenges: determining the number and style of caskets to order and from which manufacturer, figuring out the best way to approach the grief of a set of young parents, and determining how to earn and maintain a good name for himself in the community so that an entire population might trust him to manage completely these raw, difficult, and socially important moments in their lives.

Splashy trade publications like *The Casket* and *Sunnyside*–which later converged into one magazine–helped young Stephen George make these decisions. The tabloid-sized pages gave voice to the ambitious mood of the funeral trade in its early days in vivid print and illustration. Fiery opinion pieces competed for space with eye-catching ads for hearses and caskets and embalming fluids. The ads made bombastic claims or masqueraded as articles. Behind it all pulsed the drumbeat of progress and modernity. For example, a letter to the editor in a March 1898 *Casket* decries the "old fogy ways that still cling to" a good number of Kentucky undertakers who had refused to learn embalming or to sell manufactured caskets–insisting instead on the "deficient" homemade variety.[3] The editorial line was a bit hazy in this publication containing all sorts of ads for the latest manufactured caskets, vaults, and so forth.

The pages were rife with brand-new inventions. Another issue from the same year contains an ad for a patented metal chin supporter–to keep a dead jaw from dropping open in the middle of a viewing–and a number of competing burglarproof vaults. And then there's the patent notice from an Ohio man in the July 1880 *Casket* for the "Coffin Torpedo," which would fire a missile at any would-be grave-robbers. As a safeguard, the torpedo included a "rod [that] extend[ed] to the surface of the ground[,] to prevent any accident when filling the grave."[4] How exactly this safety rod would prevent the torpedo from wounding innocent gravediggers is not explained. Perhaps the weirdest ad, though, is a half-pager that features a photograph of what first appear to be a couple of scarecrows. Upon a closer look, you realize that they're two exhumed corpses, apparently a woman and child, all desiccated and sticklike. G. H. Hamrick's Embalming Liquid is the responsible party. The ad's copy brags that the bodies were infused with his magical potion ten years prior. Says the proud underlined copy: *"You can make mummies with it."*

Trade magazines also boasted professional how-to stories like Joel E. Crandall's 1912 breakthrough feature in *The Sunnyside*, in which he submitted a brash new concept called "demisurgery" (later renamed "cosmetization"). Before, the primary aim of embalming had been to harden the body to a rocklike texture in order to preserve it as long as possible, á la G. H. Hamrick's mummy-making potion. But Crandall proposed that embalmers might consider a different goal: through the use of makeup and other materials, he wrote, he had found a way to erase the physical evidence of a violent death, so that family and friends might "look upon their loved one again" before burial.[5] It sounds very much like the Victorian ideal of the Good Death. However, later critics–people like Jessica Mitford and advocates of green burial–are harsher in their assessment. To them, "cosmetizing" a body means the funeral industry's attempt to erase real death from our experience of it.

Funeral directors don't see it that way.

Deep tradition matters and so does progress, and if there's anyone in Greenville, North Carolina, who's aware of this, it's Stephen George's grandson, third-generation funeral director Don Wilkerson. This is how Don gives you the facts about progress: "It seems that Greenville might be the center, in eastern North Carolina, as far as health care goes." His tone is polite, his word choice indirect, but what he's saying is accurate. Greenville today is home to Pitt County Memorial, the teaching hospital for East Carolina University's Brody School of Medicine. The town also boasts one of North Carolina's fastest-growing public universities, one of its largest convention centers, and plans for that pinnacle of any real American metropolis:

an ovoid beltline reaching some twelve miles' diameter at its widest north-south span. Greenville is one of the fastest-growing towns in North Carolina. It's just up the road from Wilmington, where I live, and also near the tiny burg where my mother grew up.

The carloads of newcomers to Greenville from other parts of the country might judge Don Wilkerson's above statement as indirect. What it really is, however, is prudent. In telling me what she knew about S. G. Wilkerson and Sons, a woman in her seventies who had lived in a neighboring town all her life used a similar style of explanation. "It's the–well, everybody knows about Wilkerson's, of course, it's the *big*, well, around here, in terms of funerals and cremations."

For the physical structure, *big* is a good word to describe S. G. Wilkerson and Sons Funeral Home: The two-story brick structure takes up an entire tree-lined block just off Greenville's main commercial drag. Wilkerson's dwarfs the United Methodist church next door and in fact looks a lot like a church itself, all beige-brick modern, that style so popular for ecclesiastical architecture in the 1970s and '80s. A magnificent stained-glass sanctuary dominates, and when early in our conversation I ask Don whether their building used to be a church, he says, not unkindly but with a hint of frustration, "No, no. We had this building built in 1975." I'm reminded of another church-that-isn't, the Museum of Funeral Customs in Illinois, a structure that similarly reads *spiritual* without actually cleaving to any particular faith. The tone of Don's comment doesn't miss its mark, either. Someone who had lived here in 1975 would have known that this had never been a church.

Don's entire thesis in our conversation today has to do with insiders–the people who grew up in and around Greenville and the small farming communities surrounding it–and outsiders, those who have arrived in recent decades, from other places. As these newcomers arrived, life changed in and around Greenville–and death, too. The decades have altered, in ways surprising and fundamental, the manner in which funeral operators like Don work and, as it turns out, the very meaning of what they do.

After observing the business the whole of his early life, Don started working here summers at age seventeen. After graduating from college at twenty-four, he returned to work full-time as a funeral director. At that time, the early 1960s, Wilkerson's saw most payments at one time of year only. "A lot of our accounts receivable were what they call fall accounts. You carried the account until fall because that's when tobacco was sold and that's when the bills were paid. Banks were the same way." At that time, a skeletal sequence of Main Streets broke up the region's flat expanse of farmland and scrub swamp. These were the little towns of Greenville and Kinston, and around them the humbler settlements of Ayden, Grifton, Winterville, and Hookerton. They were all linked by Highway 11's two lanes and stamped with miles of tobacco and cotton fields.

All that flat farmland proved a defenseless canvas for the fleet of car dealerships, fast-food joints, and shopping malls that began their unremitting march out from Greenville four and a half decades ago, when East Carolina College became East Carolina University and, soon after, the hospital began its massive expansion. Pharmaceutical research giant Burroughs Wellcome arrived in the area around the same time, as well as a number of manufacturing plants, including Dupont. In 1950, the population of Greenville and the areas surrounding it was just over sixteen thousand. At the time of my conversation with Don Wilkerson, it tops seventy-two thousand.

Such a populace makes the traffic on the town's main commercial drag a sight to behold the Friday after Thanksgiving. The malls surge like anthills with shoppers who swarm the parking lots of Panera and Applebee's and Starbucks, their Escalades and Rangers stacking up by the dozens at each traffic intersection. Around the corner and inside the hushed carpeted hallways of Wilkerson and Sons, business is the same as it is year-round. Today, four services will take place or have already taken place—two graveside, and two more in-house. As Don sits across from me in a small conference room dominated by a table of dark wood polished to a mirror-ball shine, there are at least three other conversations taking place in similar rooms around the building. In those rooms, at those tables, visitors are planning funerals, their own or those of parents, spouses, or children they've just lost. Don Wilkerson plays the straight man for such emotionally loaded conversations every day he works, discussing with people which flowers, Bible passages, music, and caskets define perfectly the lives of their fathers, great-aunts, or selves. He addresses larger questions, too. *Am I doing this right? Why did this happen? What's next?*

Don is semiretired now and works just three days a week rather than the seven days, thirteen hours per, that he put in for forty-some years. (S. G. Wilkerson and Sons does business roughly 364 days a year, closing to visitation on Christmas Eve and Christmas morning only.)

Today his dress is characteristically prim: neat silver-frame glasses and a black suit, a bright Carolina blue tie adding a spark of conviviality. The tie is like the small jokes he starts to venture about thirty minutes into our conversation. (The first, to drive home the point that death could come at any time, for any of us: "Heck, a jealous husband could shoot me!" an infectious chortle pealing out quickly before he adds, "I don't know what he'd shoot me *for*.") When he laughs like this it's surprising, as there is so much about this man that telegraphs strict propriety. However, Don Wilkerson is also a good old boy, and I mean the term in a positive sense, the way my own male relatives from this part of the country use it: as in hail-fellow-well-met. "Oh, Don? He's a good old boy."

However, Don also moves in and out of these frank discussions about death smoothly, unlike a single one of those male relatives. He himself has had his own brush with mortality–a heart attack in his early forties. He has claimed a born-again health-club fanaticism ever since. (He blames the heart attack on the long hours; he does not, overtly, blame the breakup of his first marriage on the same, although it took place at roughly the same time, both in his life and in a five-minute span of our conversation.)

———————

Counting funerals, cremations, and bodies shipped to other states, Wilkerson and Sons oversees about 650 cases a year, a strong number for a major funeral home in a growing metropolitan area this size. When the firm started in 1932, it was a small funeral home in a small town. By the 1970s, it had an on-site crematory, which was by then a common practice for elite firms around the nation. Wilkerson's also owns and runs Pinewood Memorial Park, a well-ordered ninety-five-acre cemetery near the university. In the 1950s, when the Wilkersons purchased Pinewood, cemetery ownership was a hallmark of extremely successful funeral operations. However, times have changed, and Don frowns when he brings the place up. Perpetual care is the predicament. "Problem with cemeteries," he says, his thick brown eyebrows knitting themselves together, "whoever owns it has got to maintain it. And it's a constant maintenance thing. That's a reason churches got out of cemeteries first. Then families got out of the cemetery business by selling the land."

Wilkerson and Sons is still in the cemetery trade, even though every year more and more people are opting for cremation, and more and more, those ashes are not buried in cemeteries. And then there's the upkeep: mowing and weeding and monument preservation, which gets to be expensive for an independent business, especially when you consider the fact that cemeteries in this country are not the popular draw they once were for visitors. It's hardly the mall on a Friday after Thanksgiving. It's hardly even the softly lit halls of a successful funeral home on any day of the week. Once, the Sunday afternoon gravesite visit was customary for people in communities like this. But times have changed.

Two centuries ago, I would have called Don Wilkerson a funeral undertaker; a half-century later, just plain undertaker. The term "funeral director" wasn't invented until the late 1800s. Up until around the Civil War, people specified a "funeral undertaker" when they meant someone who dealt with the dead. The world saw the dramatic birth of term "mortician" in a February 1895 issue of *Embalmers'*

Monthly: "In the January . . . Embalmers' Monthly[,] the wish was expressed that a word might be coined that would take the place of 'funeral director' and 'undertaker.' . . . We have given the subject considerable thought and . . . present the word 'mortician.'"[6]

A business like the death trade is going to involve some euphemisms. These will change every few generations or so, as the old euphemisms lose their euphemistic quality–that is, their power to make people conceive of death as something less than the scariest thing imaginable. There was the *coffin*-to-*casket* switch. The *funeral chapel*-to-*funeral parlor*-to-*funeral home*-to-*funeral service* switch. And the *graveyard*-to-*cemetery*-to-*memorial park* switch.

"Mortician" might be a riff on the reputable, medical "physician." Given the funeral trade's extremely fragmentary record, there's no way to know for sure. But over time, anything related to the dismal trade, including "mortician," takes on grim connotations. Really, there's not a whole lot more uniformity today in the professional labels of those who work with the dead for a living. "Undertaker," "funeral director," and "embalmer" tend to be used interchangeably in current embalming textbooks and trade magazines. Despite the ingenuity of the minds at *Embalmers' Monthly* back in 1895, the term "mortician" failed to triumph over all, which is good, because the publication got to keep its name. However, these days, most professionals advertising themselves these days do so as "funeral directors" rather than as "morticians." Who knows why this is. Maybe it's that pesky Latin "mort-" that calls to mind, again and again, the fact that this person works with dead bodies. Then again, that's most likely my own bias revealing itself: The comprehensive funeral director of my imagination runs the whole show, leading widows to caskets and securing flower arrangements, while the pasty, bent mortician sticks to the shadows of the cold embalming table.

As for the humble "mortuary" from whence "mortician" sprang, it's really the granddaddy of every one of these terms, having been on the scene for hundreds of years. At one point or another, "mortuary" has meant just about everything we have ever associated with death and memorialization. It holds a two-hundred-year stint as a synonym for "funeral" in the fifteenth through seventeenth centuries. This overlaps with its definition, through the nineteenth century, as a special tax paid to the church when someone died. In the seventeenth century, "mortuary" is also another word for a burial place, and it makes at least one appearance as an eighteenth-century synonym for a written remembrance–a precursor to the modern obituary. Its modern definition, "a building or room for the temporary storage of dead bodies, either for purposes of identification or examination, or pending burial or cremation," first appeared in an 1865 trade publication. As part of the effort to establish the funeral business as an authentic, even–again–medical, industry, *Casket and Sunnyside* magazine in 1936 introduced the term "mortuary science" to refer to "the theory and practice of embalming and funeral directing as a subject of academic study."

When undertakers became funeral directors and began trumpeting their very own patented products in their very own trade magazines, it was only a matter of time until home funerals died and funeral homes were born. But there were other forces at work, too. The Civil War played a huge part in moving death out of the house, an emigration that felt extremely unnatural to Good Death-loving Americans who were used to caring for their dying and dead there. Some of the first modern undertakers were entrepreneurs who hung their shingles on barns near fresh battlefields, offering to locate bodies, embalm them, and ship them home. Virginia's Dr. William MacClure advertised that "'BODIES OF THE DEAD would be 'Disinterred, Disinfected, and SENT HOME' from 'any place within the Confederacy,'" and he had his share of Yankee counterparts as well.[7]

The late 1800s was also a period when the sick and mentally ill left homes and went to the new hospitals. As the new century arrived, death took place less frequently at home–and less frequently, period, as a result of advances in medicine and sanitation. It became something that people experienced more and more often alone, and it was handled now by specialists and strangers–physicians and nurses–at places that did not resemble the home.

The moment was right for funeral directors to create a physical space of their own. The new "funeral chapel" came first. Funeral directors often ran their businesses from mansions previously owned by upper-crust families. The large houses offered social prominence, expansive living areas upstairs for the directors' families, and large basements that were ideal for embalming.

Issues of *The Casket* were peppered with glowing profiles during this time that served as how-to prototypes for aspiring young mortuary owners. A 1905 article trumpets the Frank C. Reavy Estate, in Cohoes, New York, as "a Model of Completeness and Up-to-Dateness."[8] Readers are filled in on the business's every praiseworthy particular. There are "handsome cabinets" finished in white enamel "with mirror-inset doors, the interior measuring 8 × 13 feet, and lined with black velvet," which display funereal robes for the deceased. Such fine detail, claims the story, regularly prompts the residents of Cohoes to "make it a show place to their visitors." I love this idea: *We'll round out the evening taking in a play, but first, to the mortuary!*

Moreover, what young mortician wouldn't read this piece and dream of his own such business, complete with an "attractive" exterior "finished in paneled oak, large panes of glass, with . . . opalescent borers, and no display of gruesome objects"? These magazines are filled with such profiles, each, as one publication put it, serving as "an example that may well be followed by others who contemplate the erection of a real 'Funeral Home.'"[9]

That set of quotation marks around "funeral home" belongs to *Embalmer's Monthly*, not to me, as the term was still tentative in 1915. The funeral chapel came first, and then for a while businesses were called funeral parlors, a name coming from the room in family homes where people had traditionally met with company and laid out their dead.

But then around World War I, about the time the British were tossing their widows' weeds in the name of God and country, parlors began disappearing from homes. Homemaking magazines decried gloomy "parlors," now linked inescapably in people's minds with death before the advent of modern medicine, favoring instead a new kind of space and title: the living room. Funeral operators themselves followed suit, to avoid appearing Victorian and outdated. Their businesses became "funeral homes." In later decades, when many funeral operators abandoned the old mansions for stand-alone businesses, they abandoned the term "home," too, in favor of the ever more distant, professional "funeral service." Yet most of us still think of them as funeral homes, those places where death lives.

In Greenville, Wilkerson's has been that place for decades. Back in the 1940s, Don Wilkerson's father and uncles guided the company. In the casket storage room, they would advise you on what to buy and then take a legal pad and lean it up against one of the empty caskets, all stored upright in those days, to figure your bill before shaking your hand on it. When fall came, they'd walk the invoice over to your house or place of business, where you'd sit and talk awhile. This last practice was started by the elder Wilkersons and continued into the 1970s. All these men were affable men, and all respected countywide, just like Stephen George, who founded the firm in 1932. In the early twenty-first century, we are not untouched by these facts; their contours remain. On the webpage labeled "Staff" on the Wilkerson Funeral Home website, founder Stephen George was listed first, his four sons next. "Deceased" read the bold font above their names. This is why Don tells these stories. To make the listener understand: We are here. We are sunk down deep; the deeper we sink, and further from this moment, the more entrenched we become in the here and now.

You can guess the percentage of cremations a community might have from the education level of its citizens. "Usually, university settings will lead the way," says Don. Here in East Carolina Pirate country, the number is about 27 percent–roughly 13 points below the national average for cremations, which hovers now around 40 percent. Over in the central part of the state, the University of North Carolina at Chapel Hill, founded in 1789, has arguably played a strong role in its community for much longer. There, the percentage of cremations is far higher, around 42 percent. These numbers both eclipse what you'll find in some other North Carolina counties–like rural Hertford County, due north of Pitt County on the Virginia State line, population twenty-four thousand. Hertford's cremation rate is 11 percent.

If you were to look up the term "progress" in the dictionary, you'd find something about advancement or development toward a better, more complete, or more modern condition. Look closely. There are two definitions housed in one: the "better, more complete" and the "more modern." In Don Wilkerson's personal view, the progress inherent in the growing popularity of cremation has everything to do with the latter but less to do with the former.

Wilkerson's houses the county's only on-site crematory, and it does a swift business. The display room features an attractive array of urns: boxes crafted of finished pecan and cherry wood, many adorned with artistic bucolic scenes–enough flowers and trees to chart some new forest, a place called *Expiry Woods*, maybe, which is probably the name of a real-life cemetery somewhere, some place with real trees and real flowers. In this room, I absently play the mental game of "Which might I choose if . . . ?" and settle on a simple box that looks like walnut or locust wood, burned with the striking silhouettes of a few birds–gulls?–taking flight. There are still more to choose from: delicate vases and sterling silver boxes. And Don points out a papier-mâché plate onto which ashes are meant to be sprinkled. The plate comes with a lid decorated in watercolor with pink and yellow flowers. One floats this ultimate picnic set out onto a body of water, and the lid prevents a windy day from ruining the farewell. At the moment of good-bye, the set will float out, placid and dependable, and then sink and biodegrade, guaranteeing that your father really rests in the deep of the Cape Fear River and not around the pilings of the dock you're standing on or, worse, in the folds of your own jacket.

Wilkerson and Sons makes these cremation products available, but they've placed them in a separate side room from the central casket display gallery, which holds main event status with its even more myriad personalized options. The blue-ribbon casket here is crafted of bronze, offering "the very finest in materials, workmanship, permanence and durability," according to Wilkerson's website. Other models are crafted from copper, stainless steel, plain steel, mahogany, walnut, hickory, birch, cherry, maple, oak, poplar, or pine. Wilkerson's carries two popular brands of caskets. One of these, Batesville, offers the option of the MemorySafe® drawer, where keepsakes and farewell messages can be displayed and stored forever. Personalized designs on casket panels are another option. Then there are the optional LifeSymbols®, models sculpted from acrylic that fit into the alcoves of casket corners. Think mini golf clubs, praying hands, gardening tools, even a lighthouse for the deceased seafarer.

The idea of having a picturesque death scene replete with items *like* elaborate caskets dates back to Victorian England and the Good Death. However, while such pomp was quashed in the United Kingdom in part by that nation's massive casualties during the First World War, funereal finery in the United States continued to flourish even as our own attitudes toward death changed.

In this country, even when prescribed mourning periods and weeping veils went away, the physical Beautiful Death lived on in funeral homes—and at home funerals, too. Into the 1930s, '40s, and even '50s, funerals continued to take place at home in many small towns and rural places around the country, and great importance was placed on the appearance of such events. The caskets here at Wilkerson's remind me of an exhibit I saw at the Museum of Funeral Customs displaying a typical home funeral from the 1930s. A wooden casket lined in candy-purple plush presided before a darker purple backdrop. This casket *loomed*, draped in a mile of sparkly white bunting, all of it seeming to float, dreamlike, above vases bursting with fake white and purple flowers, a veritable floral sea. The effect was dramatic. It made me stop and catch my breath. It was kind of a beautiful death, lacking only, at that moment, the death. For years and years, it was the job of the undertaker to create such a visual effect in people's front parlors. Funeral workers of the day, people like Don Wilkerson's forebears, brought to people's houses all the ingredients for a presentable service, like traveling carnival workers. Or like salesmen: The dark purple backdrop on this exhibit folded open from a suitcase to stand behind the casket for the viewing, like those old briefcases that popped open to transform into displays of fine cutlery. In the early days of the twentieth century, every single such item–from the six-foot, aubergine velour curtain with its folding metal stand, to the small clip lamp that illuminated the deceased's face–would have been brought to the house of the deceased by the funeral professional.

This period had its own stylish trends, 1930s versions of the acrylic golf-ball panels. The open upper half of the museum casket was covered with a glass sealer, a fashionable preservative measure– basically, a small, round window through which visitors could view the deceased. According to the display text, the sealer "softened the visual image of a viewing, discouraged individuals from touching the body and kept insects away from the deceased when windows needed to stay open in the days before air conditioning." Its crafters had good sense, considering occasional hot days that harbored the twin threats of insects and melty cosmetics–even though the little round window with its bolted, metal rim made the casket look a touch Jules Verne to me.

Still, then as now, there was an incredibly pleasing design element to it all, which made me think of one responsibility of funeral professionals that I'd never really considered. Once funeral directors took on the job of creating the entire service, they also took on the job of creating the presentable postmortem scene. The embalming, the lighting, everything had to be *just so*, even the casket itself, resting at an eye level ideal for viewing. And for all this, we have those Victorians to thank. Without that prototypical home deathbed scene of heavenly homecoming before a loving family audience, there would have been no purple-plush-lined casket, no personalized casket panels of praying hands clasped together for eternity.

An even better modern counterpart to the *Twenty Thousand Leagues* glass sealer is the Cadillac of vaults. Most cemeteries require vaults, those concrete or metal boxes that enclose caskets and cremation urns once they're in the ground. Although vaults were originally invented to fend off Victorian grave robbers, cemeteries today require them because they keep the earth from settling into the grave. There are several vaults on view here at Wilkerson's, though it's nothing compared to the multiplicity of vaults displayed on the funeral home's patiently detailed website, where I count no fewer than fourteen different varieties, everything from the triple-reinforced Wilbert Bronze to the lowly Continental concrete model.

Don takes pride in showing me their very finest specimen here in the big display room. In the spot where your eyes first naturally rest sits a dome-topped model fashioned completely of galvanized steel. "It's an air-sealed product," says Don, tapping the shining chamber with pride. This vault resembles a giant silver bullet; it looks missile-like in its sturdiness. If the vault were any larger, it would resemble the bunker where I'd want to be in case of nuclear apocalypse–although I'd have to bring an oxygen tank, since it's designed not to let anything in, especially not the two enemies of preservation: water and oxygen. "And that casket, once it's in that vault, is in the *air*," Don says, gesturing again with his whole hand for emphasis. "There's not room for anything to get in there. It's tested at the factory in six feet of water, and warrantied against the intrusion of water. Most funeral homes, you'll find, don't have the capacity to inventory and to install it."

I'm left thinking of the technical raison d'être we often hear for vaults, to keep cemeteries looking golf-course beautiful, and this other reason that dominates Don's sales pitch. Body preservation. We don't have dust to dust here. We have, in some cases, dust to mummy. It is true that funeral homes make the bulk of their income from casket sales, and if you buy a casket, you pretty much have to buy a vault. Hear those cash registers.

Sort of.

Because there is more at work here than profit motive.

In the urn room, dwarfing the small funerary boxes with their flowers and trees, an actual cremation container leans against the wall. It's exactly like a coffin-shaped office storage box, made of white cardboard, specially treated. ("It must be able to contain bodily fluids," says Don.) Across the lid, in green sans-serif print, the words "Name," "Date of Death," "Gender," and "Age at Death" stand out in bland, blameless, horrifying veracity. Several finer cremation caskets made of wood repose in more traditional positions here as well, but something about the severity of this upended model says, *Interested in cremation? This is what it comes down to. This, in the end, is what it's all about.*

There's something at work in these layers of history upon which we sit here in Greenville, North Carolina. Don says nothing outright that can be construed as a personal opinion about the practice of cremation. What he does say, though, is telling. "On our side, in funeral service, there's always been a couple of things that went on." He places the tips of his fingers together as he speaks. We are back in the privacy of the conference room. As he glances up to find his words, the overhead fluorescents dazzle his glasses for a moment, and I can't see his eyes. "One, maybe if you don't look at the death, maybe it didn't happen," he says. "Have you ever heard anyone say, 'I can't believe that Joan is dead'? Well, maybe they didn't go to the funeral, but seeing is believing. The body in a casket. That's how infantile, sometimes, we are. People naturally shy away from it. It's 'Oh, I don't wanna see that.'"

But maybe they should. He never says this, but the words hang in the air, as legible as though he'd taken an indelible marker and written them on a pane of glass between us—and before we get to Don's anecdote about this, I'm going to interrupt with one of my own.

In *The Puritan Way of Death*, David Stannard describes the harsh conditions of seventeenth- and eighteenth-century New England, a time and place in which, besides accusing one another of witchcraft, the nation's earliest and cheeriest settlers also saw fit to pass the time warning their children about their likely imminent demise and hell. Constantly. In the seventeenth and early eighteenth centuries, dying was no shrouded surprise to anyone; even later, by 1850, some twenty-two to thirty-four of every one hundred infants did not reach a first birthday. It was truth in advertising when children were advised, in sermons like one by Cotton Mather, to "Go into *Burying*-Place, CHILDREN; you will there see *Graves* as short as your selves. Yea, you may be at *Play* one Hour; *Dead, Dead* the next."[10] Fun fact: Mather spoke this sermon at a child's funeral—that of fourteen-year-old Richard Hobby, who was "crush'd to death by a cart falling on him," according to a diary account.[11]

Puritan advisement on death commonly had to do with what children—and all Puritans—would find on the other side. One famous (or infamous) children's sermon by minister Jonathan Edwards described the spectacle on the infernal side of the veil this way: "How dreadful it will be to be all together in misery. Then you wont play together any more but will be damned together, will cry out with weeping and wailing and gnashing of teeth together."[12]

Such admonitions weren't meant simply to keep children in line; Puritans believed in Predestination, which meant that they had no control over their ultimate fate. *Everyone* feared eternal damnation.

By the start of the nineteenth century, the outlook had changed. Parents still talked to their kids about death and children still witnessed an awful lot of it, but in the new optimistic evangelical era, the faithful were guaranteed a place in paradise. In short: If you believed, you were heaven bound. Now, at least publicly, death became a glorious, even eagerly anticipated state. It meant reunion with lost loved ones rather than eternal separation. The Good Death was born. Stannard writes, "It was becoming the . . . accepted norm, for the godly to die 'in Raptures of holy Joy: They wish, and even long for Death, for the sake of that happy state it will carry them into.'"[13]

So what does death "mean" today? In this pluralistic society, it depends on whom you ask. Recent surveys suggest that most Americans believe they're going to heaven after they die. At the same time, fewer and fewer of us are reporting an affiliation with any organized religion. There is no single prevailing societal take, and individual, non-faith-based analyses frequently tend toward the foggy. With child mortality as low as it is, there seems little point in scaring small children or ourselves by ruminating on something that we are all so sure, in the backs of our minds, happens only to old people, a group becoming, with the elevation of medical and living standards, less and less Us. Stannard writes that more often than not, death is never really addressed to children—or to the rest of us—as a real event at all. I'm talking about not the deaths of movie villains, but yours and mine.

Stannard goes on to condemn this way of thinking. We've become a society that avoids and denies the existence of death, he says. Hence, the sterile, inhospitable hospitals in which so many people die.[14] He has a point. Think of the often lonely conditions of our euphemistically termed "rest" homes, or the sanitized portrayals of violent events by U.S. news: American television coverage of the Iraq War or of any other conflict compared with that of, say, European networks. For U.S. viewers, the human face of real death always manages to take place off camera.

Compared to the Victorian era's prescribed black mourning period and dress, grieving today is somewhat abbreviated. In his essay "The Reversal of Death," French scholar Phillippe Ariès describes a "mourning curve," or arc of emotionality through the decades in our attitude toward death. He describes the nineteenth century as "a period of impassioned self-indulgent grief, dramatic demonstration and funereal mythology"; now, he says, we are experiencing a trough.

Even in our closest friends and loved ones, we brook very little "dramatic demonstration." Instead, we expect expressions of grief to take place in private.

Blame it on etiquette queen Lillian Eichler and her ilk of yesteryear; grieving today is nothing compared to what it was in the 1800s. Then again, we may no longer be dwelling in quite the "trough" we were in when Stannard and Aries penned their complaints in the 1970s. After all, Don Wilkerson's town of Greenville, North Carolina, is home to at least two hospice-care facilities–places that champion the opposite of emotional avoidance of the Grim Reaper. Many such places encourage the living to pay their respects both to those on death's door and to those who have just walked through it. By championing comfortable dying in people's homes or in homelike settings, in fact, hospice might be the new Good Death. The National Hospice and Palliative Care Organization reports that in 2011, hospice care shepherded about 44 percent of all U.S. deaths.

Then again, other evidence suggests that maybe we're avoiding death more than ever. The rate of direct cremation–that's cremation with no service and no viewing–has risen even further since the days of Stannard and Aries, as have memorial services without the body, "to which," as poet and undertaker Thomas Lynch derisively wrote, "everyone but the dead guy gets invited."[15]

If anyone's uncomfortable with seeing real death here today, it's me. Visiting the urn room, but especially the casket room, jars me ("casket" being just a euphemism after all for "coffin," and it's not so very far from the unnerving visual of *coffin* to that of bodies and thoughts of one's own and the impossibility of Null and Never, and the memory: those childhood middle-of-the-night death panics and my father's attempts at comfort, hands stroking shoulders as if to verify our presence at that moment, his and mine, always with the final refrain, "Not for a long, long time"). It is what makes me feel strange even talking to a funeral director, realizing every two minutes the things he sees every single day.

I'll just say it, though it unnerves me to do so: As I write this, I am a death virgin. (Knock mahogany, walnut, hickory, birch, cherry, maple, oak, poplar, and pine.) My father lost his younger brother when he was a child, and he doesn't like to discuss it, nor does he harbor an ounce of interest in cemeteries, funerals, or my current preoccupation with both. Then again, I have a friend whose father died a few months ago. He brings the subject up frequently, analyzing it from all angles, and every time we talk, he presses me for any new details I've dredged up in this particular death trip of mine. He can't get enough. I have friends who find cremation—those flames, that conveyor belt—horrifying. I have other friends who shudder at the thought of whole-body burial in the ground.

You can only understand how someone else needs to handle death in the given, specific moment. There are few hard and fast rules. I understand both my father and my friend. Or rather, I understand neither and so allow both the dispensation the ignorant should grant the wise. The postulate that we have become alienated from death can be argued in the abstract, with timelines and wholesale societal evidence. And maybe on the whole it's true. However, even after analyzing our own conventions, we are to some extent stuck inside them, as I am stuck to today's popular view when talking to my father and my friend: that no matter who you are, you cannot tell someone how to *do* death.

Not like you used to. Don tells this story.

In 1972, they were demolishing the old bridge that links Contentnea Creek to Highway 11, over in Grifton, to build a sturdier one. I perk up and nod when he says this. I know this bridge. I cross it every time I go to my grandma's.

"And this guy was from Aurora," says Don. "Somehow, he got killed in the bridge demolition." It's something of a jolt, from the familiarity of the bridge over that swamp-kneed creek of my childhood, to death. Somehow I keep forgetting that over the course of this conversation with Don, a given anecdote will always lead to the main character facing a freak accident, a heart attack, or an ocean drowning.

Don continues: "These people, they were not churched. She wasn't from Aurora. This gal was about, I don't know, twenty-eight. Anyway." Anyway, this gal, who remains "this gal" for the remainder of the tale, went to a funeral home in nearby Kinston. She told the director there that she wanted to have her husband cremated. The director refused, and then he lectured her on why cremation is neither proper nor smart. Don nods as he says this, like this is a conventional course of action, to tell a potential customer, *No. You're wrong. That's not how it's done, and you'll regret this move.* At the time, it was.

Well, he tells me, this gal sat there and listened to the funeral director's advice and then stood up politely and left. She called a Methodist minister in town who then called Don and said he didn't know this gal from Eve, nor did he know what to do. So S. G. Wilkerson and Sons arranged for the cremation. There's more: When Don told this gal to bring in a nice suit of her husband's for his actual cremation, she refused, since the crematory flames would destroy the suit and anyway it was not like she would even be present. That's where Don himself drew the line. "And I said, 'Now, listen. There's a right way and a wrong way.'" In the end, she brought him the suit. Then, just before the cremation, she decided that she wanted to see her husband's body for a moment after all. "Seeing the body *meant* something to her. She didn't *think* that before."

This anecdote is a layered one, with multiple theses: First, Don's saying that in order to grieve properly, we need to see our loved one dead, to connect the vacant body with true absence. His subtle opposition to cremation goes deeper than base salesmanship; he believes in the traditional funeral as a rite that has meaning to people in grief. Then there's his second point: This is the brand of disarray you'll see in a woman without a church, a people. This is related to point number three: This is what our world has come to. It's a world in which families aren't "churched," and a world in which women no longer value dressing their dead husbands well to send them off properly from this world.

Finally, it's a world in which the funeral director no longer has final authority. The story marks a turning point in Don's life, an occasion when he served as arbiter of both propriety and desire. For most of the twentieth century, a funeral director's responsibility was defining the proper course of action for people locked in their deepest stages of grief and helplessness. Now, his role is to appease the desires of such families, no matter what those desires might be and no matter his personal feelings. The funeral director is no longer a social institution. Like so many other things, the position has become, instead, a consumer resource. Hence the paper plates for cremated remains, and hence the crematory itself, which, unlike the cemetery, comprises a greater percentage of Wilkerson and Sons' earnings each year.

And this is Greenville, North Carolina, a town seated like so many across this country, at the crossroads of old and new. It is a place of contradiction, absolutely an up-and-coming center for health care and manufacturing, but also a fairly small rural town where family roots run deep. An informal Internet search also turns up two mosques, one Jewish congregation, one Hindu congregation, and ninety churches in Greenville proper. There's Baptist, Assembly of God, Christian, Church of Christ, Church of God, Free Will Baptist, Methodist, Pentecostal Holiness, Presbyterian, Reformed Evangelical, nondenominational, and a smattering of Wesleyan, Seventh-Day Adventist, Lutheran, Episcopal, and Catholic congregations. In the small towns and rural areas surrounding Greenville are seventy-seven more churches. This is a land of small roadside signs reminding you that Jesus is Lord. It's also a land where about 40 percent of the population consists of married households, and where the median household income is around $31,000. In descending popularity, Pitt County residents work in textile manufacturing, health care, and retail industries. In greater Pitt County, agriculture, specifically soy and cotton farming, is still a big deal. And although the university, the hospital, and the pharmaceutical companies are attracting college-educated employees, the formal education of most Pitt County residents stops with high school diplomas. The vote on the 2012 election went to Barack Obama here, but by a slim margin: 53 percent.

Don Wilkerson is an avid golfer, a fan of health-club circuit training, and a joker, too. He is met with surprise by a lot by people who find his personality to be more *vital* than they expected of a funeral director. Some of his jokes run toward the bawdy. He's not above explaining his business philosophy to a Young Lady Writer, for example, with an allegory passed down from his father. "He said, 'Son? You have a business and you treat it like a lady? You put it up on the pedestal, you admire it, you treat it gently, and you give everything and you take last? Your business will look after you. But on the other case, if you treat a business like a whore, you take everything from it, you won't have much.'"

Like his family's business, Don Wilkerson fits inside the social and historical milieu of this land as a Russian doll is seated in its shell, following both its progress and its history exactly. He can point first to his grandfather, the charismatic coroner, followed by the next generation of owners, his father and uncles. All belonged to different churches—Don can tell you which—and were, respectively, a Kiwanian, a Rotarian, a Lion, and a member of the American Legion. They bought cars at different dealerships and sat on different civic boards, every single one of these moves motivated by both real community investment and marketing savvy, each a son grasping a thread and weaving his own upstanding reputation and that of the business into the community's fabric. The same can be said of Don's generation and that of his children. Always a staff of three to four funeral directors; always a Wilkerson.

When we're through and he walks me out, he recommends a good new Thai restaurant up in Chapel Hill, if I should find myself out there anytime soon. Then he shakes my hand and gives his regards to my grandmama. Outside Wilkerson's, the sudden bright sun and sounds of Greenville lunch-hour traffic overwhelm for a moment, before I regain my bearings and head out into the mundane world.

Lenette Hall,
Owner, The Urngarden

The Business at the Back of the Closet

Lenette Hall is a pioneer of enterprise. She puts it like this: "I sell the product that nobody wants to buy." As CEO, owner, and sole staff person of The Urngarden, Lenette sells funerary urns and other memorial accessories online, where she also blogs about the death trade's ever-widening world. Her company, which she started in 2000, was one of the first to sell containers for ashes directly to people, without the funeral-home middleman. She also sells her urns wholesale, to crematories, funeral homes, animal pounds, and pet cemeteries. Absolutely anyone can click through her website and buy a periwinkle marble urn—or a biodegradable shell-shaped urn, or a flag case and urn set—without setting foot in a funeral home.

"Everyone thinks that they're the only ones who've had their mothers' ashes in the closet for five years. And they're so embarrassed. They feel really bad about it. And I tell them, you know, it's pretty common. That after several years, you're finally ready to make a decision about what you're going to do."

The real truth is that Lenette sells the product that everyone wants to buy. She can barely keep up with business. She went full-time a few years back, but now, just like any entrepreneur–say, the owner of a traditional funeral home–she works even more hours than that. She spends fifty, sixty hours a week monitoring her website and talking to customers and vendors all over the country, all while pacing "The Urngarden's World Headquarters," her cluttered home office. She says she still hasn't figured out how to answer when people ask her how business is doing. "I mean, do I say, 'It's great!' with a big smile on my face? I don't know. But it *is* great."

When you think of the word "urn," perhaps you think of a huge vase, perhaps a huge, ugly vase. While technically the dictionary definition of an urn is a large round or "ovaloid" vessel used to hold funerary ashes, in the commercial funeral world the term has been expanded. The term "urn," when spoken by funeral directors or people like Lenette, refers to any object containing cremated remains. Even a necklace pendant shaped like a small silver ring, containing only a fraction of an ounce of ashes, is listed on Lenette's website as an "urn necklace." As for the big ugly ones, those are part of the reason she went into business in the first place: "The selection at most funeral homes just was so pathetic."

Lenette's favorite urns, her Egyptian line, are among her pet-owning clientele's favorite, too. Two of her most popular urns feature the ancient animal gods, Bastet and Anubis. A lot of urns resembling the feline Bastet go to bereaved cat owners. Anubis the jackal was, ironically enough, the Egyptian god of embalming. He so resembles a German shepherd that a lot of grieving dog owners snap up his likeness, and she sells many Anubis urns to pet crematories and animal pounds, too. It is, in fact, the pet urns that really launched her business. Someone whose cat, dog, or rabbit has just died is less likely to call a funeral home.

Instead, he or she scours the Internet for ash-disposal options and finds businesses like Lenette's–businesses whose bedrock is not tradition, but improvisation. Like a lot of the items she sells as funerary urns, her first Egyptian model was originally a container intended for something else–in this case, a scarab-shaped jewelry box she found for sale at a different website. She bought it, converted it, and resold it at a higher price.

Converting, the process by which an ordinary container becomes a funerary urn, is shockingly simple. The route from jewelry box, or pasteboard hutch from Hobby Lobby meant for holding TV remotes, to urn, is this: Place the ashes inside. Glue the lid. (Or, in Lenette's case: Provide the glue and instructions for gluing.) Often, it entails adding some personal touch, a little plaque or an engraving with the deceased's name. Lenette is doing nothing illegal by selling an item she buys at Kmart as something else. "If I don't do it," she says, "somebody else will."

There's a certain dizzying freedom here. Anything can be an urn. There are no governmental or international regulations regarding containers you can or can't store ashes in. None for who handles them, either. You don't need to call in a specialist to pour ashes into a container. All that you, prospective customer, need to know is contained in these words, from the description on countless Urngarden products: "Can be sealed with household adhesive for added security." Box plus Krazy Glue equals urn.

There are just a few rules of thumb for the would-be DIY funeral civilian to familiarize himself with. First is the golden mathematical precept repeated again and again on The Urngarden website: One pound of body weight equals one cubic inch of volume. Accordingly, a full set of adult ashes will usually fit inside a two-hundred-cubic-inch-capacity urn.

Although The Urngarden sells urns for human beings and for pets, its website layout for the animal deceased is slightly more straightforward. There are three sizes of urns for pets, which you can browse by clicking on three photos. "Small Pet Urns" reads the caption beneath a photo of a collie and tabby cat cuddling on a bed. "Medium Pet Urns" reads the type beneath a squinting bulldog, and "Large Breed Pet Urns," beneath a large mutt frolicking on a beach.

There is no corresponding website feature for the human deceased of different sizes.

If you're planning on scattering ashes, a smaller keepsake urn, shaped like a small egg or maybe a piece of jewelry, will hold up to three cubic inches of cremated remains. There are cloisonné keepsake urns, crystal keepsake urns, angel statue keepsake urns crafted from crushed marble, and necklace pendant keepsake urns. There are keepsake urns crafted from bronze and pewter and brass and ebony and keepsake urns crafted from honeywood, mahogany, or economy fiberboard. Tiny angel thimble-shaped keepsake urns come wrapped in snug velvet cases. You might guess, from the huge selection of keepsake urns, that jewelry containing the ashes of the deceased is extremely popular. It's true. A century and a half later, we are back to the *memento mori* of the Victorians, with our ash-containing earrings and pendants and the chains around our necks.

Maybe this time these hold a slightly altered meaning. For example, specifically Christian imagery doesn't sell as well as Lenette initially predicted. "Praying hands, and things of that nature, not so much." She allows that the customers who might go for such traditional religious images might also be inclined to choose traditional funeral-home burials. This is not to say that people purchasing urns do not yearn for some sense of the sacred. It's a delicate dance for Lenette's business to respectfully acknowledge the spiritual quality of death, while remaining completely abstract regarding the nature of that spirituality. It's the funeral homes that look vaguely like churches all over again. How does Lenette strike this balance? What *are* people looking for?

"That is the question," says Lenette. "Because we're really breaking out of the whole traditional burial style. You know what the fastest-growing religion is? No religion." It's true. A recent Pew study reports that Americans changing their religious status to "unaffiliated" outnumber new converts to established religions by a margin of more than three to one. Our widespread lack of buy-in to traditional faith is nothing, by the way, compared to the areligious nature of our international peers. In Great Britain, the birthplace of the Victorian Good Death, only about 11 percent of today's population routinely attends a religious service, and nearly three-quarters of all deaths result in cremation. (Interestingly, many more Britons than Americans report belief in near-death experiences and ghosts.) By comparison, here in the United States, nearly 40 percent of us engage in some sort of religious fellowship each week, and about two-thirds of us still choose whole-body burial. But our pew-warming numbers are dropping, and our cremation numbers are rising.

Traditional funeral homes don't particularly like what Lenette Hall does. Which is: to offer the same product they offer directly to their prospective customers, usually without such a large markup. Even worse, with cremation gaining in popularity, direct businesses like The Urngarden are pretty much pulling the rug out from under funeral services on their fastest-growing product.

"Look, they hate me," she says, "but what I really want is to work with them." She's made inroads with a few funeral homes, but "it's been slow. I encounter a lot of rejection. I'm like, 'I'd love to help you, but you *have* to get over yourself.'"

She means the funeral homes that refuse to return her phone calls, and the others that refuse to address the rise in cremation by offering a decent selection of urns. She sees how it's a bit of a catch-22. Urns just don't make as much money as caskets, embalming, and vaults. The product that has really risen in popularity in recent years is the biodegradable urn meant for scattering ashes on the water. "It's the bane of the funeral director. Because I sell a scattering set for $69. If funeral directors sell those, they're not gonna make much money. So I totally get why they're upset."

They're not just upset with Lenette, of course. Her one-woman business is but one ripple of an enormous tidal wave in today's funeral world. There are dozens of online funeral businesses like hers. Sites with names like Final Embrace and Final Reflections sell everything from teddy bears made from the clothes of one's beloved dead to professionally written obituaries, to premade wooden and steel crosses that can be purchased and placed at the site of a fatal accident.

She's not their only competition, either. In recent years, Walmart, Sears, Costco, and Amazon have all begun selling caskets and urns. This has affected Lenette, too. "Competition has gotten *steep*. I used to sell my urns *on* Amazon," she says. Not anymore.

There's one thing that independent sellers like Lenette have over the corporations, and that's personality. Behind their blogs, Facebook pages, and Twitter feeds, you can see that these are real people. They solicit the opinions and stories of those in the market for their products. On Lenette's website, she posts stories about the latest trends in the funeral industry, and readers will write in with trends or oddities that they've noticed. Sometimes she'll also post entries about completely unrelated topics: about the king among haircuts, the mullet; or about her personal king among rock stars, Eddie Van Halen. ("You know you are getting old when your favorite '80's rockers are either soon to show up on the cover of the AARP or are having hip replacements.") You read her blog and you start to feel like you know her. Unlike the stereotypical stiff undertaker of the popular imagination, her professional persona is undeniably human: informal, chatty, and completely no-nonsense.

In the funeral business, you hear a lot of people expressing true devotion toward their work. Real funeral directors, the actual nonstereotypical people who have devoted their lives to this trade, will often refer to it as a calling or destiny. It is one of the few industries in which people still spend lifetimes–providing comfort by invoking a sense of permanence when mourners are in the thick of the ultimate reminder that everything is fleeting. In the midst of all this, Lenette Hall might represent something new: an infiltration of this world by the transient.

Because she says she probably won't stay. She spends hours each week talking with bereaved people on the phone, and hours more just contemplating human cremated remains: how, for example, to sensitively recommend an urn that keeps better when buried under five feet of Georgia clay, or how to tell complete strangers that no, it's okay if they cry. Or if they don't. "This is *good* work," she says, "but it is *work*. I'm able to help families out, and I do enjoy it." She pauses. "But it's not fun. It's just sad."

Lenette began The Urngarden as a business experiment twelve years ago, and although it has roared to life with success, she's less than completely comfortable with what she does. She feels strange, for instance, creating Facebook posts as Urngarden, "because who wants to see *that* in their newsfeed?" She has lost friends over what she does–not anyone she was very close to–but it has happened again and again, and it's enough to smart. "They see me as some sort of vulture, you know? Preying on families. Which totally isn't true, but usually, when people ask me what I do, I just say 'Online retail,'" or 'I'm in Internet marketing.' Because once you tell them [the truth], *that* shuts 'em up!"

I first met Lenette in 2008. Her business was doing well then, too. Still, at the time, she told me she was probably going to shut the business down soon to go do something else. Now, five years later, she says the same thing. Maybe.

She laughs. "You know, my husband asks me, what would I do? And truly, I don't know. Not death and dying. But I don't know. I'll tell you, this Urngarden has been one of the weirdest things that's happened to me."

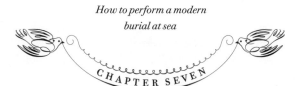

CHAPTER SEVEN

With the Fishes

Ryan Jackson knew just what he wanted when his time came. Old-fashioned burial at sea was his plan; his casket would be ceremoniously jettisoned off the side of a ship and into the deep. Ryan loved the water. He was a Vietnam vet–a marine. Before then, as an adolescent, he had been one of Busch Gardens' first barefoot water skiers, among the youngest the park had ever had. When Ryan died of a heart attack, his widow, Chris, investigated conventional sea burial. Among other rules and stipulations, she discovered the following, from the Federal EPA's Title 40, Volume 17:

> Burial at sea of human remains which are not cremated shall take place no closer than 3 nautical miles from land and in water no less than one hundred fathoms (six hundred feet) from (i) 27°30′00″ to 31°00′00″ North Latitude off St. Augustine and Cape Canaveral, Florida; (ii) 82°20′00″ to 84°00′00″ West Longitude off Dry Tor-

Burial at Sea, J. W. Carmichael, 1855.
The Illustrated London News, August 4, 1855.

tugas, Florida; and (iii) 87°15′00″ to 89°50′00″ West Longitude off the Mississippi River Delta, Louisiana, to Pensacola, Florida. All necessary measures shall be taken to ensure that the remains sink to the bottom rapidly and permanently.

It was all a mite more complex than she had anticipated, and so when a little more Internet research turned up the site for Eternal Reefs, their offerings struck Chris as the next-best option.

Eternal Reefs is a company that mixes the cremated ashes of your loved one with a cement compound to create part of an artificial coral reef. The company encourages survivors to participate in the creation of the artificial "reef balls" and to oversee their final deliverance into the ocean–the modern-day version of burial-at-sea–at one of several dedicated offshore reef beds.

Year by year, more and more people are scattering or burying cremated remains in places of natural beauty. A couple of decades ago, the National Park Service, recognizing an unstoppable phenomenon when they saw it, came up with a system of permits and guidelines for people who wanted to scatter ashes. Among the requirements on the Grand Canyon's application: "No teeth, bone fragments, or remnants recognizable as human remains may be scattered." At Yosemite, "cremains must be spread over an area large enough that no single portion is accumulated in one place." Last year, Rocky Mountain National Park fielded 78 such requests (that's up from 25 five years before), and the Great Smoky Mountains National Park in North Carolina and Tennessee, 106. And this doesn't begin to count the people who scatter first and ask questions later.

This country has seen its cremations more than triple in the past thirty years. To a people increasingly turned off by burial–whether it's due to an aversion to the body's natural decomposition process or to the time, effort, and planning that burial requires–scattering in places of natural grandeur offers the same sense of reunion with the earth. What higher tribute is there, after all, than to infuse a place of natural, indisputable majesty with someone's remnants forever? What higher praise than to endow someone's very identity with the power and beauty of that place? The red walls of the Grand Canyon become your grandmother. The ocean, your husband.

I'm not sure what mood to expect at one of Eternal Reefs' two-day reef-ball-deployment events. I'm hazarding: a funeral service with reefs? But when I shake George Frankel's hand at Friday's reef-ball viewing—he's a hardy man with a rough-hewn sort of Brothers-Grimms-ish countenance—he pulls a lopsided grin at my outfit. "Ah, dressed carefully. Very conservative, very good," he jokes, and he's right. I chose a gray nondescript top, black pants, and pearl earrings this morning. Now I'm standing in a wide, fishy-smelling alleyway. The six mourning families who are congregating wear vivid sundresses, shorts, and T-shirts as they chat away brightly over bottled water and sodas. George Frankel and Don Brawley—Eternal Reefs' CEO and founder, respectively—wear khaki shorts and tidy logoed polo shirts, sea blue. The spirit here is not at all funereal, despite the preponderance of dark sunglasses on this overcast, muggy morning. Instead, far-flung family members greet one other with the warmth of long-awaited reunions. Small children abound, as does purse rummaging for baggies of Cheerios, juice boxes, and toys.

There is a tamped-down sense of thrill in the air, the sort brought on by novelty. The hulking objects of this fascination sit crouched in a neat line on the other side of the small lot. To visualize the artificial coral reef balls, picture circular footrests made from gray cement. Now picture those footrests shaped like hollow bells: round on top, flat on the bottom. Two to four feet tall, and just as wide. Their surfaces are peppered, Swiss-cheese-like, with holes and remind me in appearance of nothing so much as the trick-or-treater in the Charlie Brown Halloween Special who dressed as a ghost but cut four or five too many eyeholes in his sheet.

Tomorrow, these families will take a chartered fishing boat out on the Atlantic and watch as the reef balls are placed at sea. There, as part of an artificial reef, they will help support a vital and endangered ecosystem. Tomorrow we'll be careening across turquoise water, the wind whipping our hair. For today's viewing, though, we're standing in a featureless alleyway off Shem Creek, the major waterway to the ocean from Mt. Pleasant, South Carolina. The sandy lot smells slightly of brine and is sandwiched between two boat storage units: a squat shed and a tower of metal girders stretching two stories into the sky.

Soon, the families are mingling around the reef balls, which are more or less identical in appearance but contain the ashes of people who were, in life, complete strangers: fathers, husbands, grandfathers, and in one case, a cat named Mistofeles. Wives and sons and daughters snap pictures and reach out with tentative affection to stroke the reef balls as they murmur over the pretty bronze plaques pressed into each.

The flat brass plaques are engraved with the deceased's name and dates. The whole package really makes me think of headstones, and I have to remind myself that they're much more than that: these objects *are* the deceased. In a way, these survivors are interacting directly with the bodies of the people they loved in life, although most probably prefer not to think about it that way. Funeral director Don Wilkerson's comment flurries through my mind: *Have you ever heard anyone say, "I can't believe that Joan is dead"? Well, maybe they didn't go to the funeral, but seeing is believing.* I wonder how much this physical contact also results in a kind of "believing," a tangible step in the long process of what people today call "closure."

(Later this same year, Eternal Reefs will change their design, so that rather than being spread through the entire reef ball, the cremains will be concentrated in one teardrop-shaped cement "pearl" in the center. The change expedites the entire reef-ball-crafting process, so that families who come together for the deployment can also be present for its creation earlier the same weekend, rather than having to shell out money to travel to two separate events. When I first hear this, I'm a little disappointed at the loss of direct interaction between mourners and the deceased: Looked at one way, the post-2007 memorial reefs are mostly just monuments *to* the dead, rather than transformed versions *of* them. On the other hand, more family members now get to interact with the ashes: pouring them into the mold for the pearl and decorating a new cement ring around the reef ball with handprints, for example.)

A woman here today from Georgia tells me that she counts among her life's worst memories the funerals she remembers from her Italian American childhood. "Corpses in the house, and everybody screamed and yelled and carried on, and at age five or six or seven, that makes you fearful. And the *corpse* was in the *house*; can you imagine that?" The mood here is comparatively sedate. No corpses in anyone's living quarters, nor, as someone else here puts it, "the ashes on your mantle that you have to feel creepy about." These families have come here to usher their loved ones, quite literally, away.

Beyond the small plaques affixed to each, the families have personalized their reef balls in other ways. Ryan Jackson's daughter tells me that while his was still a wet cement and ash mixture, her mother had mixed into it the following: locks of hair from his grown children, several of his military ribbons, a Green Bay Packers' Cheesehead charm, a small Egyptian ankh he'd made (he was a jeweler), and a tiny pair of ruby red slippers "because there's no place like home, and to her, my dad was home." Most of these cement balls also sport, carved into the surface, the initials of grandchildren, brothers, and wives.

Eternal Reefs' founder Don Brawley is, at heart and in background, *not* a funeral man, but "a reef-baller from way back." He's most interested in undersea ecosystem preservation; this interest started in college, when he and some diving buddies noticed that pollution, human contact, and temperature disturbance were causing some of their favorite reefs in the Florida Keys to look as if they suffered from massive cases of tooth decay. Don has dedicated much of his life to developing the reef ball, this object made of cement and special additives, on which real coral will grow and thrive. Like many driven people, he's happiest when attending to the activities most closely related to his passion: actually making the reef balls, or talking about the new plant and animal life he saw flourishing around a particular reef on a recent dive.

Don's demeanor is quiet and unflappable. I wouldn't call him a people person—he's not one of those gregarious beings to whom others flock naturally—but he is good at calming family members of the deceased and at making them feel useful. Today, I see him collect several people who seem at loose ends and put them to work. He charges them with making sure their family members sign in when they arrive or has them distribute crayons and paper to children so that they can create rubbings of the bronze plaques. They are small tasks, but people take them up eagerly.

Grief itself might be physically intangible, but people like having activities that create a tangible *something* out of this abstract emotion—especially activities that make us feel like we're helping shepherd life away from life. Even small tasks, like giving out crayons. "One of the key things that we do," says Don, "that I don't think anybody else in this industry does, is we get the families involved." He's talking about the funeral industry—not the industry of turning people and pets into coral reef balls. His is the only company in that particular industry. (Two companies come close: Great Burial Reef creates hollow artificial reefs that you can pour your loved ones' ashes into and seal shut at home. And the Neptune Society has established an underwater reef "city" off the coast of Miami in 2009. Planned eventually to span sixteen acres, this "classical re-creation of the Lost City, 40 feet under the sea," resembles the crumbling Atlantis of a 1950s pulp novel cover, complete with "bronze statues of lions, majestic columns and sculptures of shells and starfish." Cremains are placed in cement molds of "decorative features" shaped like starfish or shells.)

We homo sapiens like the idea of somehow endowing one's temporary stay on this earth with permanence in death, even if that permanence means a resting place where the living person couldn't have survived for five minutes in life, a place ten miles out to sea and fifty feet below it. A lot of people here tell me their loved ones were scuba divers or sailors who felt more at home by the ocean. One woman tells me her husband didn't want to be in a cemetery at the top of some lonely hill. "At least he'll have fish visiting," she says. And when the artificial reef does deteriorate, "his plaque will fall down to the ocean floor and the sun will shine on it."

Many of these families held traditional memorial services months ago. This weekend holds a slightly different meaning for them. Call it Memorial, Part II. This is one of the advantages cremation has over traditional burial; it gives survivors the benefit of time. When grief's first sharp horror has dulled some, it's easier to think creatively enough to figure out the ideal memorial.

"Ed, Dad, Poo," reads the plaque on the reef ball that's garnering the most photos at the moment, that last word being a typo. So says Jennifer Dolan, the thirty-something daughter of Edward Dolan, who died last fall of colon cancer. "Yeah, they left off the 'h.' 'Pooh' is what the children called him."

I swear there are at least eight or nine children swarming in a bee-like blur around this reef ball, although actual fact places the real number at five. Jennifer is personally responsible for four of the kids: two sets of twins who inhabit that golden age just beyond toddlerhood. They've been making colorful crayon rubbings of their grandfather's plaque, and now they're in the process of really discovering the reef ball in terms of its full potential as a jungle gym. Its many small holes serve as wonderful cave openings in which to pour sand, and, as they're now finding out, even better footholds. It's official: The artificial reef ball bests the funeral urn when it comes to real entertainment value. Jennifer Dolan and her sisters clasp hands over their mouths and look around in ambivalent delight as the children clamber all over their grandfather's reef ball, just as they used to do with the man himself when he was alive.

A few minutes later, it is really hot and thick, and George Frankel walks to the center of the lot and announces that it's time for the military honors. Eternal Reefs staff will arrange and host the honors if any of the deceased merit the ceremony; there are four this weekend. And it's interesting: Even though the boats that deploy the reef balls don't set sail till tomorrow, all the families–even those whose dead were not veterans–have turned out for today's ceremony, too. It's as if membership in this particular set of mourners trumps their own personal mourning.

Army, Marine, and Air Force service members have arrived and have spent the last fifteen minutes staking out three corners of the gravel lot. As if to show up the others, the Marines, dressed in blue, are already standing at strict attention. Among the families, sunglasses come out.

George Frankel reads aloud the names and military honors of each veteran as each honor guard performs its intricately choreographed ceremony. Beside me, a man whispers to his young son, and seemingly partly to himself, "And it's not a *real* shoot. It's just a *pretend* shoot. And I'm not sure what the symbolism is for the shooting. I don't know." He pauses and looks up at the Marines in their pressed and starched blues. "Maybe we can look that up. When we get home, do you want to do that?"

The boy doesn't really respond. He's watching with the open-mouthed concentration of a toddler as the Air Force honor guard snaps to attention, whisking their M-1 Garand rifles skyward as one. A few minutes later, the Army guard members perform their own intricate choreography, and a baby-cheeked, stone-faced soldier presents a folded American flag to Lesley Cullen, whose husband Bill won several awards for his service in Vietnam. Her eyes widen some as she steadies herself and swallows hard. It's like watching a woman who's not used to having doors held open for her. I scan the lot for Kathleen and Damian Leopard. The parents of Mistofeles the cat are standing at one corner of the squat boathouse, looking on with expressions of interest and conviction.

Four times the service members go through their formations and shoot into the air, and four times, a serviceman holds a bugle to his lips and "Taps" is played. I find out later that it's a recording, but in this moment, it sounds nothing less than immediate. They must march past Dumpsters swarming with gulls, and sometimes around steel pillars and cement pilings. Of course they do this with aplomb. It is their job, and their unflappable countenances come across by turns, to me, as professionalism and slight disdain for the unorthodox setting.

After the last honor guard hands over the last flag, Don goes to the center of the lot and claps his hands. "This concludes the presentation of military honors," he says. In seamless transition he then reminds everyone that they can purchase "some of the best shrimp in South Carolina" at the shrimp house of Wayne Magwood. This is Magwood's lot we're standing in.

While Don talks, the families are fanning themselves with their programs. An Airman quietly approaches one of the wives and presents her with the spent shells from the military salute. She nods and accepts them and then spends the rest of Don's talk staring down at them there in her hand.

It's been close to two hours in the muggy, dusty heat, and Margo Dolan, gray-bobbed matriarch and widow of Ed, a.k.a. "Pooh," is fanning herself with one of the morning's green paper programs. She tosses me an easygoing smile as she leans against her car, waiting for her offspring to round up their own offspring. Tomorrow looks to be smooth sailing; she's checked the weather report.

"So we don't have to worry about motion sickness. They say there's only one time someone got really, really sick on one of these trips. They were *convulsing*. And they had to call the Coast Guard to get them!"

Considering that every Eternal Reefs voyage means rounding up a group of potentially emotional strangers and putting them out to sea on a hundred-foot fishing boat together, the odds of witnessing at least one dramatic event seem pretty good, I say.

Margo sees it differently. The fact that it's a group event lends it an emotional stability. "In fact, it's kind of strange, but since all these people are doing the same thing, you feel kind of a camaraderie."

Half a year ago, when her husband died of cancer, things were different. "Since Ed was sick for so long, when he died, I just wanted some space for myself." They were living in Louisiana, where they had no immediate family, and the prospect of organizing a funeral in the midst of her own grief was just out of the question. "The funeral thing is a hard thing," she says. "You've just lost a loved one and then you have to go through all that stuff that is not natural for you to be doing: going to the funeral home, standing there, greeting everybody, making the small talk and making all the decisions about, you know, the body and the coffin and everything." Margo thought she'd feel guilty about her no-funeral decision; she waited for that feeling, but it never came. Just before he died, her husband signed off on creating a coral reef ball with Eternal Reefs.

Everyone here seems to be haunted by memories of some funeral past, and Margo is no exception. "I had," she takes a deep breath, "a brother who died when I was young, and that was just the most awful time for my parents." She's gone with Eternal Reefs to avoid "the special cars, and the procession and the opening of the grave . . ." She straightens up. "You know, it's just not for *me*. Maybe some people get comfort out of that, you know? But there should be another option, and this is a wonderful option."

Her family arrives. We wave good-bye, and then she disappears into a blue station wagon and is gone. The lot is empty again, save for seven concrete reef balls that stand alone, still stones in the shade of the dusty lot.

On land, the artificial reef balls are awkward, unwieldy, and extremely heavy beasts. Like penguins or porpoises, their true beauty and potential are best grasped when viewed in their natural habitat: at work in the salty deep. A cable television special captured dramatic footage of artificial reefs that had spent a full decade on the ocean floor. Covered in algae and plant life and eroded some with the years, they look organic; beautiful and worn and almost ethereal in that way of organisms of the demersal deep. At 235 to 4,000 (yes, 4,000) bottom-heavy pounds each, the reef balls are built not to budge. Don Brawley tells me he's performed follow-up dives to check on colonies of reefs they've placed in spots where hurricanes have blown through. Not a one has ever moved. One selling point is the fact that the reefs are designed to last more than five hundred years. That's far longer than most traditional graves.

The next morning at the dock feels like summer camp. Shorts and T-shirts abound, and the air holds a sense of imminent adventure. Small children are stopped and rubbed down or sprayed with sunblock. One pair of toddlers wearing Barbie and Spiderman life vests chase each other around and around the wooden walkways.

Eternal Reefs has chartered two fishing boats. One is loaded with the seven artificial reef balls, and the other, the 110-foot *Thunderstar*, will carry the six families (one of the deceased has no family or friends here today) and founder Don Brawley. About five miles out to sea, the boats will rendezvous, and there, the reef balls will join about seventy others some forty feet below on the ocean floor.

That is what is supposed to happen, if everything goes according to plan. Of course, the sea being what it is, and Mother Nature being what she is, events are not so smooth on every voyage. Sometimes it's stormy and the excursion must be canceled altogether. On other days, the weather appears fine, but the sea is too rough to lower the reefs properly. The families have been told about these possibilities and they know what to expect. Already today, things are running late. We were supposed to be off by eight o'clock this morning, but that time comes and goes. Half an hour later, instead of any stressed-out fits or other signs of the impatient need for control that can take hold of people in funereal situations, this group remains remarkably relaxed. They're swapping fishing and diving stories—or, like Bob Allen, looking out quietly at the water.

Bob Allen is one of those white-haired seniors you just know could take you in an arm-wrestling match. He's hale. He has these great teeth. And there's something else: A nimbus of thoughtfulness and alacrity that feels magnetic here in this bright morning sun out on the dock. He's also freshly the widower of Diane Allen.

"I'm seventy-two," is the first thing he says. "I met her when I was eleven, so that's sixty-one years ago. We actually grew up together and went to school together. About a year after graduation from high school, we got married. And were married about fifty-two years. Little over fifty-two. It was an amazing, amazing period."

He sounds astonished, like he's recounting something he himself has just learned, and his voice grows increasingly hoarse with emotion as he speaks, but he doesn't stop. He talks about their three children and all the places they lived in California, his wife's painting and all the eccentric people her art appreciation brought into their lives. Except he doesn't pluralize that last word. "Life" is what he says.

He pauses here. "I mean, it was nothing really complex." And a couple of minutes later: "It was nothing really interesting." But then he'll say, after a longer pause, "It was just an extraordinary life." His work as an engineer allowed the couple to travel. Nothing really great, he says. He tells a story about traveling to Denmark in the dead of winter. "And I mean, it was absolutely frozen!" But the couple used the opportunity to take a train to Sweden and back. "It was just incredible."

By "incredible," he means the trip to Sweden and the opportunity to travel in general, but also the quality of their trips together and the whole of Diane's life, which was his life as well until recently. Tears now run freely down his face, but he continues talking, gesturing as he does. They frequented the ocean and the mountains. They hiked. They scuba-dived. "And we lived by the ocean the last third of our life." He wipes his cheeks finally, shakes his head, smiling. "Through it all, it's been a remarkable life." And there, he stops talking.

———

It's time to board. As quickly as that happens, the boat leaves the dock and we're zipping down Shem Creek in the direction of the Atlantic. Over one hundred feet in length, the *Thunderstar* looks majestic from the outside. Being a passenger makes me think of something a friend once said about New York City: So vast, so little personal space. There's a covered aft deck and a long cabin lined with booths and tables. Atop this sits another, larger roof deck. There's also a narrow walkway that traverses the perimeter—but as on most sea vessels, each of these spaces, save the roof deck, feels snug.

I head straight for the roof. It's a stunning view. As we depart, we watch the blue that surrounds us widen in the morning light until it's an unbroken expanse but for the green strip of land retreating behind. It feels like we're flying. Another fishing boat zips past us, speeding back toward shore. Gulls and pelicans fan out like a pennant behind it, undulating en masse and diving for fish in the long slipstream.

Lesley Cullen and her mother, Penny, watch our own boat's wake. Lesley's husband, Bill, died last August from a brain tumor. He was fifty-eight. He was also, as summarized by Lesley, a building inspector, a skier, a scuba diver, and a master woodworker. But what Bill Cullen was most proud of was his job in the water rescue squad on New Jersey's Passaic River. He was also a Vietnam vet and a firefighter. A busy man. "Oh, yeah. He did everything," says Lesley, rapidly chewing her gum. She talks fast. An energetic blonde in her early fifties, she's attractive in the sinewy, bronzed way of women who spend a lot of active time in the outdoors. As she talks, I envision a closet at her home devoted to wetsuits and skis and those hiking backpacks with frames.

After Bill was diagnosed, Lesley says his fellow firefighters threw a big party in his honor, "with lots of beer. He was a Budweiser lover, and loved to party." When he died, Lesley says they had "the big-deal fireman's funeral with bagpipes and everything."

"And that was what Bill wanted," she says, talking rapidly. "But this is what he really, *really* wanted, I think." Final rest in the Atlantic Ocean. In addition to four other places: Lesley has also scattered or buried Bill's ashes on his favorite Vermont ski run, underneath the apple tree in their backyard, in the Passaic River, and below the window of his building-inspection office, "because he liked to be everywhere," she says. She wanted to scatter in Jamaica, too, "but I was afraid the airport sniffer dogs might stop me."

In its creative variety, Bill Cullen's last wishes have a lot in common with those of many Americans. Right this moment, dead Americans across the continent are getting made into diamonds and ink drawings. A business in Illinois will make you into actual plant fertilizer so that Aunt Maggie really can feed her favorite rosebush for years to come. Another company, called Celestis, will shoot your ashes out into a victory lap around the planet for less than it costs to fly to London. "Today we are opening the space frontier for all of us," announces the website of their partner company, Space Services, Inc. In ten years of business, the company has flown the cremains of hundreds of people, including James Doohan (that's Scotty of *Star Trek* fame) and one of the original Mercury Seven astronauts, L. Gordon Cooper. After-death experiences marketed toward lifelong passions are way up in the sky and down in the dirt—and they're multiplying.

And while most new memorialization options seem to involve ashes, some do not. If the family of Mistofeles had decided they wanted to hold on to a lifelike version of their cat, there's an array of companies willing to compete for their business. My favorite is Perpetual Pet, a freeze-drying service. Unlike taxidermy, pet owners who opt for freeze-drying reclaim their entire pet, rather than just its outsides molded over an artificial form. "This allows pet owners to see, touch and hold their pets," reads their web copy, "and in a sense, 'never have to let go.'" It's true; Perpetual Pet's site is full of photographs from satisfied customers, of their Persians, Pomeranians—and even one lop-eared rabbit—all seated in lifelike poses. I just can't stop thinking of the extra dimension this would add to one's life. The explanation to new visitors. The dusting.

———

"And it's amazing," said Eternal Reefs' George Frankel, "how few funeral directors have even thought about it. I mean, they're selling keepsake jewelry and stuff like that, but they don't take it to that next step and say, 'Okay, how much is there out there that we can offer these families?'"

There's the memorialization business, which is this geyser of new innovations, and then there's the funeral business. Ninety percent of funeral homes across the country are still family-run independents, passed from father to son and daughter, and largely, the dismal trade is still a conservative one, based more on tradition, trust, and insularity than on openness, supply and demand, and innovation.

Like other entrepreneurs trying to break in, George Frankel finds this to be excruciating, especially when he compares it to enterprises like his own. The funeral industry, he says, is "one of the stodgiest businesses I have ever seen," although he does concede that there's a gulf of trust to be bridged between the traditional service and businesses like Eternal Reefs. "And this I understand. 'How do I know who these guys are, and am I going to turn my families over to them?'"

Increasingly, the answer is, "Sure." Now that Eternal Reefs has been around for more than a decade and has enjoyed spots on the Discovery Channel and in the *New York Times*, more people are walking into more funeral homes and saying, "My father loved deep-sea fishing. What's this reef thing I've heard about?"

Something's working. And it's about a lot more than the allure of thriving coral, the brilliance of a dramatic painting (ArtInAshes. com), the sparkle of a diamond pendant (Lifegem Memorial Diamonds), or the attraction to any of these products created from ashes. There's also repulsion at work: that modern discomfort many of us feel when we're presented with a dusty old urn up on a mantle filled with cremains. Or a cemetery. Americans lead lives that are increasingly transient. You may live out your toddler-through-teen years in a small mill town in Washington state, but chances are you will not still be there when you hit thirty. Today, the average person might call three or five cities and towns "home" over the course of a lifetime. Meanwhile, our siblings and stepsiblings are leading completely separate geographic journeys. So it's not exactly shocking that the enduring phenomenon of the family burial plot, that after-death "home," is in decline. Only about a third of all cremations are interred in a cemetery, and there's no precise research about the destinations of the other two-thirds. However, consumer options for scattering ashes are skyrocketing, and national parks are reporting an increase in the number of permits requesting to scatter. Increasingly, our eternal homes are those multiple places that have moved us and given us refuge throughout our lifetimes: our backyard gardens, the Atlantic Ocean, the Passaic River.

Halfway to the spot where we'll deploy the reef balls, it's time to decorate the tribute memorials, announces Don Brawley over the boat's loudspeaker. Like many good inventions, the miniature tribute memorials came about as a result of near disaster. It happened on one early Eternal Reefs voyage. The day was sunny and bright, but the seas were turbulent. They sailed to their appointed spot several miles out and waited for the water to calm. And then they waited some more—and bobbed and swayed and waited. Turned out the water was too choppy to lower the reef balls at all, and it looked like the entire trip—with its invested plans, hopes, and plane tickets—was a bust. It was then that Don spotted one of the small-scale models he'd brought on board to show people. They're the same mushroom-cap shape as the real reef balls, with the same holes, but small enough to grasp in two hands. "And I said, 'Since we can't put the reefs out, why don't we give all the families the reef models and let 'em decorate them with the flowers we have on the boat? And we can still give them closure to this.'" On every voyage since, they've done this: decorated the small replicas and ended the day by dropping them overboard. The invented ritual now has a name—the tribute memorial ceremony—and having been so named, has acquired the feel of a rite: at once organic and traditional.

The families, mostly the women, gather on the covered aft deck. There, the small reef-ball replicas wait on a table ordinarily used for cleaning fish. Next to the table are buckets filled with roses of every color, carnations and daisies, lilies and black-eyed Susans, baby's breath and daffodils. Some women set right to work in the manner of expert flower arrangers, trimming stems and placing blooms of complementary colors and heights into the small holes—as if sticking flowers into miniature artificial reef balls were something they passed the time doing for every special occasion. Some of the mothers gather with their kids on the floor of the boat, where the work is more haphazard and wild, and soon the entire aft deck is a riot of stems and leaves and blossoms of violet, pink, crimson, and green.

Don has tasked me with decorating the tribute memorial for Richard Paraska, the man without any family here this weekend. I start braiding daisies and peach-colored roses into a chain, which I loop around and around the concrete replica. There is no single good method, but we all stick to this assigned arts-and-crafts project with avid concentration. As we work, I am struck by a feeling of historic parallel. A hundred years ago families would wash their loved ones' bodies. This piece of concrete I'm lavishing with purple, crepe-papery statice and pink alstroemeria has nothing to do with Richard Paraska. But because we humans are so good at conceiving of the transubstantial, at assigning symbols and stand-ins, what we are doing, what *I* am doing, becomes a modern version of that old process, several times removed.

Soon, the lonely-looking replicas are transformed; the most embellished resemble bouquets, and they all look something like Easter, that time of renewal. I stick a few more sprigs of greenery into mine and stand back. It's one of the simpler memorials, but it's pretty. I hope I've done Mr. Paraska justice.

The families have retreated to the boat's various corners as we zip across the open water. Now the *Thunderstar* makes little leaps across the waves, and it's a bit of a job to maintain one's balance. Inside the

cabin, everything vibrates with the thrum of the motor. I steady myself by holding on to the back of one of the booths that line the walls,
stopping to fix my eyes on the horizon out the window. It smells in
here–like port-a-potty disinfectant and plastic and salt and fish. All
these strong sensations, the motor's dull roar, the smell, and the jostling, take up a lot of immediate attention and it's hard to remember,
at every moment, why we're all here. Ten minutes ago, we were decorating the tribute memorials, but now everyone's snacking. Small
coolers appear. People get their food and retreat back to their family
groups.

We bounce along the three-foot swells and then we're slowing and
then we're idling. We've reached a spot that resembles every other
spot around us exactly, except that here, forty-five feet below, there
is a colony of man-made reefs. About a quarter of a mile away, we see
the other boat, the one carrying the artificial memorial reef balls.

White-haired Bob Allen wends his way toward me, laughing as he
grasps at railings to steady himself. I ask how he's doing. "I'm doing great! I'm doing great," he says, and he looks it. The open sea air
seems to have crystallized a hardy relish about him.

Don announces over the loudspeaker that the reef deployment
will begin shortly, and people crowd onto the rear deck with cameras
and children slung around their necks.

Laws vary by state, governing how Eternal Reefs can place its reefs.
South Carolina has designated a number of artificial reef sites,
stretches of seafloor with flat, sandy soil that are relatively close to
other so-called "live bottom" areas, in order to attract sea life. The
site we're adding to today has been there about six years.

The state program's raison d'être has nothing to do with Don
Brawley's mantra of emotional closure and reef preservation. Instead, it's about commerce. Later on the phone, the state's artificial
reef coordinator, the amiable Bob Martore, tells me that instead of
considering things like preventing coastal erosion, "we try to space

the sites out so that people with differently sized boats can access them." This site's location, some five miles offshore, makes it a really good fishing spot for smaller boats. This final memorial and resting place, from South Carolina's point of view, is basically a fish nursery. "And it does prevent overfishing in other live-bottom areas," he adds. "We're just putting down structure that acts as a substrate for the type of undersea community that would inhabit this area anyway."

Here's how this state-regulated structure–that is, the artificial reef containing the remains of your Uncle Nick–transforms into the picturesque organic wonderland splashed on every page of Eternal Reefs' website. Once it's placed, the artificial reef attracts hundreds of tiny creatures, the soft corals that cling to and encrust its rough concrete surfaces. Hydroid corals look like tufty white dandelions up close; en masse, like those giant star-like firecracker bursts. There are bryozoans and also encrusting sponges. Then come the barnacles, oysters, and tiny, antennaed porcelain crabs that live inside the reef's soft folds and crevasses. Next, the small swimmers arrive: the fiercely defensive blennies, who use their lips to scrape algae from hard surfaces, and the myriad species of gobies that feed upon all these creatures. Next in the chain are the slightly larger porgies, pigfish, and grunts, and finally, the chief quarry of fishermen and the reason for this reef's existence: king and Spanish mackerel. Spotted sea trout and redrum, black sea bass, zebra-striped sheepshead and silvery-gray spadefish. Forty feet below us, about the height of a four-story building, a reef built of some seventy manmade balls upholds an entire bustling ecosystem.

Back on the surface, there's only the rolling gray-green water. The *Thunderstar* bobs in circles. The second boat's crew seems to be bustling around with some rigging. It's not clear what they're doing, but whatever it is takes ten minutes. On the family boat, people fall into private conversation, and a few disappear back into the air-conditioned cabin. Every few minutes, Captain Leary starts up the grumbling motor and maneuvers our drifting vessel back into place. It's beginning to smell like diesel fuel here on the aft deck.

Bob looks at me and shrugs good-naturedly. "Well, only time will tell," he says. Some minutes later, Don gets back on the loudspeaker. "I believe our guys are now ready. Our first memorial reef will be Diane L. Allen." Don repeats her name a second time. It sounds rather like he's paging her, and just like yesterday when he announced the shrimp for sale, there's that strange impersonal feeling. Then again, my account is rapidly becoming unreliable since I'm concentrating hard on maintaining a bright outlook, which hinges on my maintaining a chicken biscuit, coffee, and juice in their proper places in my digestive tract as we bob and sway, bob and sway.

We watch as the crew on the other boat secures Diane Allen's reef ball to the rigging and swings it out over the side. Bob's face is a map of heightened emotion whose complexity cancels out any one simple expression, a balloon filled almost to bursting.

They lower Diane's ball into the water, but then it comes back up. This happens again, and a third time. (Later, Don tells me that the mechanism they use requires that the line go slack in order to release a reef ball. "In the area where those reefs are, we tend to have some pretty good currents, so that was part of the problem. And then the release mechanism itself got twisted.") The moments are fraught with an increasing sense of drama; it seems uncertain whether this process will work today.

All at once, the terms created for this weekend swirl around my brain, divorced of their meanings. Tribute memorial, reef viewing, reef dedication. *Solemn things*, my brain tells my body. My body doesn't care. It has rebelled. Quickly, I make my way back toward the cabin and gesture toward the paper bags piled there; a man standing in the doorway hands me one with wordless haste. The sack is comically narrow and the boat is jostling so much that it seems like trying to use the bag would defeat, and then gleefully mock, the purpose, so instead I just head for the end of the boat farthest from the families and lean out over the side, where, as inconspicuously as possible, I lose my breakfast directly over a colony of beautiful undersea memorial reefs.

When I get back, they're still trying to drop Diane Allen's reef ball. Inside the cabin, a number of people sit hunched over or sprawled out in the booths. They are pallid and silent. One seasick woman hasn't left the toilet stall since the boat first stopped over the reefs. Feeling slightly better now myself, I grab a bottle of water and head back out on deck.

Diane Allen's ball is still being lowered and raised. At one point, it *clunks* against the side of the boat, drawing gasps from everyone. Finally, it goes down into the water again and the claw-like hooks that held it emerge empty. On the loudspeaker, Don announces a successful deployment and people applaud. Bob's family members hug one another, and he wipes his eyes. He catches my eye and winks, bittersweet.

The next couple of reef balls go down without a problem, but then on the following two the same repeated raising and lowering occurs. The reef ball for Bill Cullen, that jack of so many trades, is one of the last to go, and it takes the crew a very long time to maneuver it into place. I am sitting on a water cooler by the cabin door with a cold water bottle across my eyelids when I hear Lesley shout in her quick, birdlike voice, "Budweiser!" Seconds later, there is a small cheer as the ropes emerge from the water empty, his reef placed. Lesley is ecstatic, bouncing by and pulling out her cell phone after she and her mother grip each other in a quick hug. "You won't believe it," she tells the person on the phone, her sister. "They just lowered his reef, and it was being a pain in the neck. Took, like, twenty minutes! Because it was Bill, being difficult. And then I said, 'Budweiser,' and off it went. Of *course!*"

The final reef, belonging to Mistofeles the Cat, is lowered without incident.

The heat, the boat's pitching, and the seesawing suspense and relief of the last hour and a half have all been trying. Yet attention refocuses quickly for the Tribute Memorial Ceremony. Don again announces each name over the loudspeaker, and wives and husbands (and in one case, owner) toss their small beflowered models into the sea. It's an activity that embraces the families, again, with the reassurance of participation. There is no depending on the mood of the ocean, the functionality of rope-and-pulley systems, or fishing-boat crew. There is only the feel of concrete in hands, and then letting go and watching as the small, adorned ornaments disappear into the waves.

The last tribute memorial is dropped, and Don reads an excerpt from the speech by John F. Kennedy that talks about our ocean origins: "All of us have, in our veins[,] the exact same percentage of salt in our blood that exists in the ocean, and, therefore, we have salt in our blood, in our sweat, in our tears. We are tied to the ocean. And when we go back to the sea–whether it is to sail or to watch it–we are going back from whence we came." It's a stirring moment, and then it's over. There's a click and a hiss over the loudspeaker, and Don says that this concludes today's memorial reef dedication. Less than a full minute later, Captain Leary starts up the boat again, and we gather speed. We travel fast, faster than on the way out, skimming atop the water headlong into the clean air. A few sickly faces emerge from the cabin, and the fresh wind evaporates the sweat from them. They join others who stand aft, put their arms around one another, and watch the wake we churn up and abandon, tracing a path from them to their past that is soon obliterated by the rolling, tossing waves.

Anne Gordon,
Funeral Chaplain

Funerals Are Fun

Every pew in the chapel at Andrews' Mortuary was packed. An eighty-three-year-old retired fire chief, veteran, and family patriarch had died in his sleep. His helmet, bronzed, rested on a stand next to his open casket, which was draped with the American flag. "Some among us," Chaplain Anne Gordon told those assembled, "are called to protect and to serve. These people choose difficult work. To them, it is challenging, and also infinitely satisfying."

When some people operate in their ideal role, they become dazzling. Others sort of disappear, blending, chameleon-like, with their position. Anne Gordon is a creature of the second variety. She becomes the job of funeral chaplain, and it's impressive to watch. Only when she discusses it later, say, while gesticulating over her half-empty mug of Earl Grey the next morning at the local big-box bookstore, does talking about her job fill her with a pronounced vitality. "I love it!" she says, chipper. "I like doing funerals!" She takes a sip of her tea, thoughtful. "I don't like doing weddings so much. People weep and expect all these things, you know. Get hysterical and stuff. Funerals? You know: they come in, they sit down, they cry, they leave." Her enthusiasm bubbles over into laughter. "It's great. I *love* doing *funerals!*"

Chaplains are autonomous ministers who serve in hospitals, prisons, the military, and other settings where people experience physical and emotional crises. They must know their flock, must gain their trust; a Navy or Marine chaplain will march twelve miles carrying a forty-pound pack alongside the soldiers. However, chaplains are always separate from those to whom they tend, always independent. Chaplain Gordon works with, but not for, Andrews Mortuary, and her motivation is simple. It's not about growing a congregation, only about ministering to people in times of suffering.

Anne Gordon is five foot two or three. She wears sensible silver-rimmed glasses and, when delivering a sermon, nondescript gray trousers. Her copper-highlighted graying hair is cut in a practical bob. When we first meet, I think, incorrectly, that if she were to have a pop-culture counterpart, it would be the mild-mannered and deferential Marcie from *Peanuts*. And then she starts talking, and every single thing she has to say, even mitigated by her soft Glasgow burr, shows that I was absolutely wrong.

When she's not conducting funerals, Gordon volunteers part-time as a police chaplain in Leland, North Carolina. She loves accompanying patrolling officers on their twelve-hour overnight shifts. No one on the force pays her, and she answers to no boss. As a result, officers feel free to talk with her about anything without fear of professional backlash. Sometimes it's books or sports. (Football is another of Chaplain Gordon's major passions, but she doesn't choose sides. "I'm very ecumenical. I will cheer, 'Get the ball! Get the ball!' and then I will say to the other guys, 'Get 'em! Get 'em! Get 'em!'") Sometimes, however, conversation turns to the grittier stuff of police life or to spiritual questions. She pauses for the perfect words before leveling a blunt stare. "I'm a safe place to fall. They know they can come to me and talk to me about anything, and nothing is repeated." She likes the unpredictability of this job, how some nights are quiet, while others are not. "To me," says Anne, "it's exciting. High-speed chases are exciting, I think!"

As a girl, Anne Gordon wanted to be in a man's world. That's how she puts it. Specifically, she wanted to follow her father into the British Navy. But options for women in 1960s Glasgow ran more to "work in a bank, work in a store, be a secretary, be a nurse, or be a teacher." She ended up working as an ER nurse, a job whose short, intense commitments suited her. "You deal with a situation, then you leave. I like that." She says chaplaincy is a sort of spiritual nursing. She diagnoses and treats the bereaved or traumatized, prays with them, talks with them. And then she's off.

When the funeral home calls on Anne to do a service, the first thing she does is contact the family to arrange a time to meet a day or two before the funeral so that she can prepare the service. When they meet—she and the widow or grieving children or parents—she never asks specific questions. Mostly, she just lets the person talk.

"And sometimes we talk for an hour, sometimes it's two or three hours." This need of the bereaved just to talk took her by surprise at first. Now, though, she considers it the most important part of her job. People in grief are angry or numb or in shock, and while other types of clergy, like ministers and priests, have a set schedule and other responsibilities, "I can sit for hours. I can go in and say, 'Talk to me,' and if they're silent for the next ten minutes, that's fine! If it takes all day, that's fine." Her voice is quiet, but she's so emphatic that it's as if there are invisible exclamation points floating in the air after her every sentence. If Anne Gordon proselytizes for anything, it's for this acceptance of the strange world of emotion and behavior brought about by death.

It's not easy work. People come to her at their worst, and sometimes there's not much good to say about the deceased. In such cases, Anne will often recite a verse from Philippians in the ensuing funeral service. "Whatsoever is good, whatsoever is profitable, think of these," she'll tell those congregated. She adds her own bit at the end: "Let the rest go."

Her job is to help create what people in the funeral business call a positive "memory picture," the bereaved's final remembrance of the deceased. Unlike, say, an obituary writer, her job is not truth teller as much as it is peacemaker. She'll give families her phone number after they talk, and sometimes they'll call her later that day. "'Oh, I wish I hadn't said that one thing,' they'll say." And Anne will remove any mention of the unpleasant fact from the service.

She also tells families ahead of time that they can stop the service at any moment, "if they need to cry, or pass out, or get a glass of water," or for no reason at all. She believes it's because of this freedom to behave any way they wish that no family has ever interrupted a funeral. "And it's allowing those people to be themselves, allowing them to cry or swear or whatever. It's okay! If that's where you're at, that's where you're at."

Anne Gordon and her husband had lived in North Carolina for three years when God called her to become a chaplain. If you press her on the details of this decision—if you ask her, for example, When did she know it was right for her? Was there a moment when she was working as a chaplain and just knew she'd made the right choice?—if you do this, she will pause, patiently, the most patient person ever, clearly trying to gather the right words, looking away from you as she does this. Then, "Okay," she'll say. That quiet gaze again. "I've always been a chaplain." As a nurse in the ER. As a counselor to abused women at her former church. "Chaplaincy is just a movement in the same direction. It's just another name."

On a sunny afternoon, Anne Gordon stood behind the podium in the chapel of Andrews Funeral Home to begin the service for those assembled there. "Death is final. While none of us really knows what to do in times of death, we all die." Silence. She looked around the congregation, a small crowd: the stricken friends and family of a man in his thirties who had died in a motorcycle wreck just four days before. The mourners wore jeans and sweatshirts. Prior to the service, many of them had moved about the chapel in confused, somnambulant patterns. It was as though not only their friend's death, but their presence at this service, had taken them quite by surprise, death lifting them up and away from their normal lives and dropping them here, in this still and airless chapel, in the middle of an ordinary Sunday afternoon. "We all die," said Chaplain Gordon. Confident. "Every single one of us in this room, here, will die. And it's okay."

If you talk with any person in the funeral business, you are likely to hear a great deal about "service to the families," about customers' needs coming first. And it's true. The folks who pick up the bodies, those who embalm, and those who help families choose caskets and sign the proper documents and then ship remains off to the right authorities, work long hours. They get calls at three in the morning and go. They work without vacations, and their first and final thoughts of each day often involve confirming the perfection of every detail.

These are professionals, and they are concerned primarily with their professional world, a world whose placid state of being and whose survival depend on the execution of funerals, which are intricate events involving emotional people. In this business, there is nothing more important than reputation, and so you find an inevitable obsession with it. There is a *lot* of "In our business, families come first" and "In this town, our business has an untarnished image." A lot of *One-hundred-percent satisfaction guaranteed.*

The business of Anne Gordon is less self-conscious because there is no business. God has called her to be a chaplain now but, she freely admits, that may change at any point. She has the freedom many of us would like for ourselves in our own work: its motives are its intrinsic rewards alone. "I do it first of all because I love to do it. To me, it's kind of like prayer. You pray because it's there. I don't expect to see God doing great things. My job is just to pray. My job is to do the funeral. And let God take care of what he has to take care of. Stay out of his way."

In her role, she emphasizes a *lack* of control. For example, "At the start of my services, I always talk about death," she says. "And it's o-kay! It's okay to die! I notice that so much–in nursing, for example. When you're nursing people in Europe, and they're old and they're dying? 'Let them die! And let's *support* them in their *death*!' In America: 'Let's try to keep them alive for as long as possible.' And it's considered an affront to the medical society when somebody dies. So I want to break that."

The U.S. health-care system's major claim to fame is its application of cutting-edge procedures and medicines that socialized systems like Great Britain's can't afford. However, critics say that such technology has the net effect of prizing lifespan over quality of life. In a recent NPR story about this phenomenon, a British oncologist named Dr. Fergus MacBeth echoed Chaplain Gordon's sentiment: "What I see . . . is what . . . seems to be a culture of gross overtreatment of patients, of raising false hopes and putting patients through extreme treatments for very modest gains or very modest probability of gains."[1]

MacBeth's depiction of the U.S. medical system today is kind of an eerie echo of the system's early days. At the start of the twentieth century, people like Elie Metchnikoff were shaping the basic principles of modern medicine. Metchnikoff, who followed Louis Pasteur as the director of the Pasteur Institute, called old age "an infectious chronic disease," one that science would one day cure.[2]

This tenacious way of thinking, which views sickness and old age always as foes to be vanquished, may still be a significant strand of thought in contemporary American medicine. But other philosophies have sprung up in reaction. Hospice, for one, focuses on accepting an inevitable death and making it more comfortable. In hospice, death takes place in people's homes or in homelike settings. In

2011, about 44 percent of all U.S. deaths took place in hospice. The birthplace of this end-of-life palliative care? Great Britain, Anne Gordon's homeland. In those nations' ninety-thousand-some square miles, a land area roughly the size of Michigan, there are about 270 hospice centers.

Still, as far as Chaplain Gordon is concerned, the United States still has a ways to go to overcome its fabled obsession with youth and death-fearing materialism. "In America, you're never good enough. You're never thin enough. You're never young enough," she ticks off, with increasing enthusiasm. And for a moment, Anne Gordon, a chaplain sitting at a Barnes and Noble, is making loud and funny jokes about Botox and breast implants.

Does she ever get bored conducting funeral service after funeral service? No, because each person is different. And what of all those funerals—isn't it exhausting to spend day after day ministering to the shocked, blank parents of teenage car-crash victims, to the angry young widows and the broken old widowers? What of them all?

"I dismiss them," she says, after a significant pause, drawing the "I" out into brogue. "I don't recall individuals. I dismiss them. I have to! It's 'Been there, it's done, move on.'" Like a good ER nurse.

But then she pauses. Every now and then, they do get to her, she says. She has no idea why. She's tried to pinpoint it. What affects her is never the deceased's personality or any similarity he or she may have borne to Anne. It's something else that she can't quite name, so she calls it *spirit* and leaves it at that: The spirit of the deceased touched hers. A few weeks ago, she did two funerals in the same week. One was for a thirty-four-year-old woman who died unexpectedly of heart failure. The other was for a sixty-six-year-old woman whose death was also completely unexpected. Anne Gordon can't recall the cause of the older woman's death, nor any details about her life. "She didn't live any differently from the thirty-four-year-old. Yet there was something about that woman that *touched* me."

This is rare. Usually just after funerals, Anne Gordon seems lighter of heart, just on the safe edge of giddy. For example, following the service for the elderly fire chief, while his soberly dressed family members were still shuffling past, Anne approached me in the lobby of the funeral home, her pace brisk. "Okay, so how's it going?" she asked, her smile satisfied and nearly jovial.

What matters most to her is the challenge met, and who's next. To help people in their sorrow, repair what she can through compassion, and then move on.

Death by the Roadside

It was the year of the Brittanys. Four young women named Brittany had died in four separate auto accidents. The families put up roadside memorials to their girls: crosses and funeral wreaths and homemade signs. Some months later, after a local's complaint about the growing number of memorials like these cluttering the streets of the town where I lived, the state DOT cracked down. The subsequent debate led the small coastal city of Wilmington, North Carolina, to take note of all the roadside memorials that had been cropping up on its shoulders and medians for years—and to wonder what to do with them.

According to North Carolina law, any memorials placed on state roads must be out of the right-of-way. At the very least, said community officials—forced into the awkward position of arbiters of grief—the families needed to clean up their existing memorials and take home any loose photos or flowers. But this decision only generated

John Gray mourning ring. Gold, enamel, crystal, gold foil, and hair,
by unknown goldsmith, 1763. Jewelry number 0046.

more controversy. Debate sprang up in our paper's Letters to the Editor column and all over town. I wondered, too: What of the petite mountain of stuffed animals in front of the hospital on Seventeenth Street at the spot where a woman and her daughter had been hit while jaywalking? Or that half-surfboard planted in the ground for years on the road to Carolina Beach? A newspaper writer named Pat Gannon had been covering the phenomenon. He pledged to document, on the paper's website, every memorial in and around Wilmington–a new one each week, he said.

It was Gannon who got me in touch with Mary Wilsey. She was more than willing to tell me about the roadside memorial she maintained and, more importantly to her, about the daughter she lost, Brittany.

At twenty, Brittany Vidal-Wilsey was working her way through college following a rough period of, as Mary Wilsey puts it, "too much partying, drugs, you name it" in her teenage years. She had straightened out and moved back home again. Mary describes a typical day this way: "Brittany would wake up at her boyfriend's house, call me. Then go to school, and call me on the phone after her first class. I'd talk to her during lunch, about her friends, her plans for dinner, whether she'd be home, whatever. Then we'd talk on her way home." Mary and her daughter talked so much each day that their exchanges resembled one long conversation that ran for years. Mary had a houseful of kids, but she was closest to Brittany–so close that sometimes, things got a little weird. For example, Brittany? Beautiful. This girl never was without a boyfriend; she received her first marriage proposal, from a thirty-something restaurateur, at the age of twenty. "And she would tell me everything," says Mary, laughing a little. "I mean, about the men she dated. And it tended to be, what's that, 'TMI'? Too much information?" She laughs again, more of a real laugh this time. It's sort of hollow and yearning.

From the sofa in the living room, you can see two framed photos, both of Brittany. They dominate an otherwise Spartan beige wall that stretches up to a high ceiling. In Brittany's bedroom, Mary shows me photo albums, including Brittany's christening album. Framed photos crowd the bureau. In the family office, there are digital slide-shows, one for Brittany's funeral and one for the family's anniversary gathering one year after her death. Loose photos are taped to the doors of the computer hutch where we sit to watch the electronic images rotate. In every single one of these dozens of exposures–be it some aunt's birthday party, a summer morning when twenty cousins are packed onto one sofa, or some unexceptional afternoon–Brittany is smiling. She has olive skin and greenish eyes and really white teeth, all of this framed by dark, wavy hair. The girl smiles; she smiles again; she is always smiling, and not only smiling–this assertive smile, preternatural in an eight- or thirteen-year-old and dazzling in a nineteen- or twenty-year-old.

While it's true that it's Brittany's appearance I'm attuned to on this visit, it's still kind of shocking. Brittany takes over every single picture she appears in. Even in those pictures taken at the spur of the moment or when she just happened to be there. Even in the bad, blurry photos, or photos where she's off to the side, Brittany's wide open smile makes her the most physically striking person in every still, and also the most aggressive; she steals the focus of every one.

Mary Wilsey looks tired. It's a tiredness that seems stitched into her, and this is not just something I say because I know she's mourning her daughter who died in a car wreck fifteen months ago. It's the clearest thing about her. Her eyes are brown and very round and shaded by dark circles. Her long, brown hair is pulled back into a ponytail with long, feathered bangs that trail down the sides. The first evening we talk, she smokes a number of cigarettes and drinks two cans of Dr. Pepper. Her sadness is palpable. She seems broken but somehow unbeaten. There's something in her small wiry frame that harbors intensity, and this is even truer of her eyes. When she talks about her daughter, she says, "She just wanted everything." She says, "She was just a full-of-life child," and she herself is reanimated.

———————

Brittany Vidal-Wilsey's roadside cross and wreath are not plainly visible from NC 133, and I miss them the first time I drive down. "Well, I'm glad you did," Mary Wilsey tells me with a sigh, "because I need to redo it." The whole thing's looking a little worn, she says. The white cross needs to be repainted and she needs to make a new funeral wreath. She takes me to the furnished garage behind her house to show me the wreath she's been working on, one of those arrangements of artificial flowers up on a stand. Brittany's new wreath, which is about half completed, will be made of white carnations. If you buy the stand and fake flowers yourself, it's cheaper than buying the whole thing from a funeral home every time you need a new one. "And I might as well learn to just make it," says Mary. "I'll be doing this for the rest of my life."

Twenty-one miles of state road separate the small community of Boiling Spring Lakes, which the locals call BSL, from the town of Leland. Except for two gas stations, one brightly lit and one boarded up, Highway 133's two lanes glide alone through miles of piney swampland, uninterrupted until the entrances to new subdivisions start cropping up near the borders of both towns, developments with names like Olde Towne and Saint James Plantation.

Both BSL and Leland are bedroom communities that satellite the small coastal city of Wilmington, North Carolina. It takes about half an hour to drive from BSL, where Brittany Vidal-Wilsey lived, to Wilmington, her destination the evening she swerved around another car, overcorrected, and smashed into a tree. The place she lost consciousness forever is seven minutes from her house, just around the corner from the boarded-up gas station. Brittany's cousins and siblings made the cross that stands at the spot, and Mary Wilsey made the wreath. That younger generation, kids in their teens and twenties, tend to honk or wave when they drive by this memorial. Mary hopes they also take a look at their own speedometers.

Brittany Vidal-Wilsey's roadside memorial is in no official peril from the state. It's placed on the property of Orton Plantation Gardens, which has given Mary the go-ahead to maintain it there.

"Yeah," says Charlotte Murchison, the office manager at the Gardens, "she was over here, I believe, looking for her daughter's necklace? And she met our garden manager and asked him, 'Is this memorial okay?' And we have no problem with it at all." Murchison mentions the memorials for two young men who died in another accident about a quarter of a mile further down the same road. "If it brings comfort to the family, I've no problem with it. We have absolutely no problem." She repeats this several times.

Gentlemen's agreements like this, and other cases, of people sneaking unapproved onto highway shoulders, medians, and private property to nail crosses and plaques into hostile ground–these things are happening every day, in every corner of our nation. Here in North Carolina, law prohibits "all signs other than official signs" on roads maintained by the state. It also forbids people from placing "objects" on the right-of-way, which is the land surrounding the road, including the shoulder, and in some cases, the ten to twenty feet surrounding it. This law is why all those other memorials got removed earlier this year, and why Brittany's remains. It sits on private property.

The nation's roads and highways are a crazy quilt, each state struggling to create a roadside-memorial law that works both for its bereaved and for other drivers. In Wisconsin, roadside memorials are not illegal when placed outside highway rights-of-way, but they have a limited lifespan; they can stay up for only one year. In Alaska, people can maintain memorials for two years, but they must be *in* highway rights-of-way. Virginia, whose law forbids homemade memorials in the right-of-way, allows survivors to buy official state-sanctioned black-and-white memorial signs. In California, you can get an official "Victim Memorial Sign" if and only if a drunk driver caused your loved one's death. CalTran's website stipulates that "an intoxicated driver who died does NOT qualify as a victim."[1] Whether animals may qualify as victims came up for debate in 2012, when animal rights activists petitioned for a memorial at the Irvine, California, site where a container truck crashed, spilling some sixteen hundred pounds of saltwater bass. According to PETA's website, the proposed sign would read, "In Memory of hundreds of fish who suffered and died at this spot."

Here in North Carolina, where Mary Wilsey lives, the DOT balks at setting up any kind of official sign program, citing a rationale similar to California's. "There's a danger in paying official tribute," says NCDOT's Steve Abbott, to someone who died because she was driving drunk, or even someone, like Brittany Vidal-Wilsey, who was just driving recklessly. The state doesn't want to heroize such behavior.

In the Southwest, roadside memorial culture is a different animal altogether. There, memorials are referred to as *descansos* or "places of rest." The descanso, a centuries'-old Mexican American tradition, is a homemade roadside cross that helps the spirit of the deceased ascend to heaven. In 2007, the state of New Mexico made it illegal to desecrate or disturb them. It's not clear whether the rise of roadside memorials across the country has anything to do with the cross-country Mexican American diaspora or its influence. It *is* clear that people of every cultural background are creating them in every state, and if news story after news story is to be believed, they're doing so in growing numbers.

With legal decisions come debates—and sometimes lawsuits. In Colorado in 2001, a man who tore down a roadside cross in a median strip was tried for "desecrating an object venerated by the public." In his legal decision, Judge Jeffrey L. Romeo concentrated on whether the hefty metal cross was "a venerated object." His first conclusion was that the family had failed to secure proper permission to place it. He then moved to wholesale condemnation of the memorial, taking the following series of deductive steps.

> They have no authority to do that. It's state property. . . . Once it's put up, technically it is abandoned property. It is abandoned as a matter of law. . . . Finally, another statute that needs to be considered is *18-4-511, Littering of Public or Private Property. . . . It says, "Any person who deposits, throws, or leaves any litter on a public or

private property or waterways, commits littering." . . . Litter has a
legal definition, and the Court is bound by the legal definition, not
what someone may think is used in Webster's dictionary or might be
used in common conversation. It does in fact constitute litter upon
the highway. It's a Class 2 petty offense to do that.[2]

Having been thus demoted from the category of venerated object to
that of litter, the Colorado cross was removed officially and for good.
The man who had first torn it down was absolved of charges.

In Detroit, the family of Brian Generazio dismantled a "ghost
bike" memorial that someone had put up at the site where Brian, a
cyclist, was hit by a car. Since 2003, bicycle activists all over the country have painted dozens of bicycles white and displayed them at spots
where cyclists have been hit and killed by motorists. Brian's family
didn't like the ghost bike, though. They said it "intruded on their
grief."[3] It turns out that Brian himself had held an especial dislike for
roadside memorials; furthermore, his family didn't want to drive past
the spot where he'd died and see such a manifest reminder of the tragedy for years to come. Meanwhile, in his and other cities, new ghost
bikes continue to appear.

Alaska, which permits roadside memorials, reached that decision after the mother of a teenager killed by a drunk driver turned in
a petition protesting the previous law that had outlawed them. The
petition had 244 signatures. Lori Backes, staff to the state rep who
proposed making memorials legal, is quoted as saying, "This is a phenomenon that won't be stopped."[4]

There are more cases, too. Alabama outlawed roadside memorials
in the name of public welfare. ("We are trying to balance safety with
compassion," said one ALDOT engineer.)[5] And in Utah, the American
Society of Atheists claimed a court victory against the State Troop-
ers Association, which was ordered to take down a number of metal
crosses the association had placed to honor fallen officers.

Meanwhile, roadsidememorials.com, which began selling two varieties of ready-made wooden crosses in 2005, cautions customers to

check with local property owners and legal authorities before placing one of their solid oak markers. Before purchase, would-be buyers
must check a box next to this text: "Roadsidememorials.com will not
be responsible for any accidents or injuries due to the placement of
your cross."[6]

Even though Brittany's memorial is not at risk for removal, Mary
Wilsey remains eager to talk with journalists and writers about why
it's so important to her. She let one reporter take her photo next to
Brittany's cross as traffic flew by on the highway down below. "People drive down the roads," she says, "and death never even crosses
anybody's mind if they don't see one. But when you see one, it brings
death to your attention."

The memorial is for everyone. It's a reminder to drive safely. But
it's also extremely personal. It's a reminder of one particular death
and of one family's grief. It's a reminder that death happens.

It's this memento mori aspect of roadside memorials that a lot
of people just don't like, and that has sparked debates in state after
state. All over the country, you also see a lot of opinions like this one—
about a different memorial—from the online comment section of the
Wilmington Star's website.

> While I have plenty of compassion for this woman, I also see the haz-
> ard her memorial puts on the roadside. Suppose someone comes
> down the same road and is distracted by this memorial, crosses the
> center line and slams headon [*sic*] into another car, and someone
> else dies because of this woman's memorial?[7]

Safety seems a reasonable concern. It's certainly one that is echoed
in legislative reasoning again and again. In my own months of monitoring newspaper stories, I did find one accident in which it seemed
the absence of a memorial would have saved lives. Two teenagers died
in Oahu after being struck by a car while laying flowers at the already
decorated site on Kamehameha Highway where a friend had died.
However, none of the news stories I read about the tragedy ques-

tioned the wisdom of the memorial's existence or that of the teenagers who visited it. Instead, community members seemed to place full blame on Tiati Kane, the driver who hit Orem Kauvaka, sixteen, and Summer-Lynn Mau, nineteen. (Kane claimed full guilt and said that she suffered psychiatric problems, and also that she may have been "assaulted, robbed and possibly raped" shortly before the accident took place.)[8]

Here in North Carolina, a communications official with the Highway Patrol says that he can't recollect a single accident caused by a roadside memorial, though of course it's tough to know for sure. The state DMV collects some accident figures, but nothing this specific. Wrecks caused by memorials may have occurred here or in others places, but no hard and fast data prove that they make driving any more hazardous than the rising number of distracting smart-phone apps or clever Chick-Fil-A billboards.

Here's something interesting, though. Online comments for news articles about roadside memorials usually follow the same pattern: Anonymous Person A writes that homemade crosses and wreaths and signs might cause new accidents. Anonymous Person B points out that no one has ever expressed such a concern about, say, prolific election signs. Anonymous Person A, or perhaps C, says, Yeah, but memorials are an eyesore, or, Yeah, but the mourner should keep her grief in a cemetery or at home where it belongs. Like this anonymous commenter from an online discussion about an article on Wilmington's memorials controversy:

> I may not be a perfect driver, but I don't intend to shove my personal grief into anyone's face and use it as a sheild [*sic*] against law breaking.[9]

Or this, from a suburban Chicago paper:

> ALL road side markers of this kind should be banned! If you want a place of rememberance [*sic*] for your passed loved one–GO TO A CEMETARY. This is what they are for![10]

It seems that what motivates a lot of people to oppose roadside memorials, more than a bighearted concern about driver safety, is a sense of personal umbrage about public grief. With their homemade signs, photos, and declarations of heartbreak, roadside memorialists are crossing a polite societal line, one so entrenched in this day and age that no one ever talks about it: Grief is private.

In a society where this is resolutely true, the roadside memorial becomes sort of a guerrilla move. A flag planting in an unconquered space. And we're seeing more and more of the like. Mourners can now design their own memorial T-shirts or car decals. They can order rubber wristbands bearing the deceased's name or emblazon a billboard with his photograph–and they are doing these things, and inventing still more ways of announcing their grief in unexpected and heretofore mundane venues.

Historically in this land, it wasn't grief in public spaces that violated mourning propriety, but its opposite. In the 1700s, the British trend of giving out copious food, drink, and personalized mementos to funeral goers was the vogue among well-to-do and aspiring New Englanders. In those years, invitees left burials and the gatherings afterward several pints tipsier, often wearing memorial rings imprinted with the deceased's likeness. Memorial needlework, scarves, and poems were also popular giveaways. People adorned themselves and their homes with these mementos mori, which became everyday, commonplace reminders of mortality.

Most often, though, you hear about the gloves.

Memorial gloves were the memorial wristbands of moneyed eighteenth-century New England. The gloves themselves were black and their quality varied, depending on the social standing of the deceased–but it's not their appearance that's commented on in old diary entries and letters so much as their numbers. In the mid-1700s, a minister named Andrew Eliot claimed to have collected 2,940 pairs in the course of his three-decade career, and in 1736, more than 1,000 pairs of memorial gloves were given out at one funeral alone–that of the wife of Governor Belcher.[11] People of lower classes acquired the practice, and when they did, the incurred cost sometimes depleted their assets. At the 1738 funeral of Wainstill Winthrop, "the entire expense . . . scutcheons, hatchments, scarves, gloves, rings, bell-tolling, tailor's bills, etc. . . . amounted to one-fifth of the entire estate of the deceased gentleman."[12] ("Scutcheons" and "hatchments" were wooden tablets painted with the family crest or with "winged death's heads, crossed bones, picks and shovels, imps of death, and coffins.")[13]

The General Court of Massachusetts passed law after law attempting to halt the excess, but the giveaways continued. Meanwhile, several hundred miles to the south in Virginia, the problem wasn't gloves, but guns. In addition to eating and drinking away the deceased's estate at funerals, many attending Virginia funerals indulged in shooting their firearms. The popular convention so divided people that some began including provisions in their wills earmarking money expressly for funeral goers' mourning clothes–but none for gunpowder or spirits.[14]

Whether it was an excess of gloves, grog, or guns, those who opposed these practices disliked the waste they represented. But they also disliked their tone, the way they brought the profane world into what were supposed to be sacred rites. The ideal funeral was a solemn, pious affair, not a drunken, profligate revel. It was fine, desirable even, to encounter reminders of death in the everyday, but to bring the everyday into mourning's rarified realm was to besmirch it. The concern today is reversed: Daily life is not supposed to carry reminders of our own mortality. We should not have to see mourning if we don't choose to.

A couple of days after giving the okay to the hospital staff to shut off the machines that were keeping her daughter alive, Mary Wilsey drove to the flower shop to purchase funeral bouquets. She went to the funeral home too, to pick out a casket and make arrangements for the viewings and service, as well as a bridal store, to pick out a dress for Brittany.

"I went and started buying things, and everybody was like, 'You don't need to do this,' and I said, 'No. You don't understand. I have to do this; this is my child.'" Mary is speaking quietly and slowly; her voice positively thunders. "Nobody else knows what I want for her."

At the florist, when Mary started ordering bouquets and wreaths, she says the clerk went white, avoided eye contact, and generally just acted really nervous. "And when I left, I said to everybody, 'Was she a little uptight, or did I just sense that?'"

Mary's friend filled her in: Usually, the mother of a deceased twenty-year-old girl doesn't actually go out into the world to take care of arrangements herself. Usually she stays in, grieving, being taken care of instead of caretaking still. Mary had brought her grief to the flower shop. She had made the clerk uncomfortable.

This assessment set her off. Couldn't people understand? This was the last opportunity she'd get to take care of her daughter. She *had* to do this.

I think about this story again while Mary talks about Brittany's roadside cross and wreath by the side of Highway 133, about how she needs to remake the wreath but is having a hard time tracking down a funeral sash that reads "Daughter." Mary is such a busy, extroverted person; it must have seemed strange to her that people expected her suddenly to go quiet. I ask her about this and she thinks a minute before saying, "Okay. We were brought up that when somebody died, you never spoke about it again. You didn't bring their name up because it was rude." She refuses to go quiet with her grief now. Although she has a group of supportive friends and family, others have fallen away. "You tell people, 'My daughter passed away,' and they look at you like, 'Oh, my God. I can't talk to you anymore.'"

Although she hasn't absented herself from the world, Mary Wilsey has been living at an occupational remove. The first time I visit her, fifteen months after her daughter's death, she's just gotten a job–part-time work assisting the county Parks and Rec Department with its senior citizen program. It's the first role unrelated to grieving that she's taken on since Brittany's death. Like a nineteenth-century mourner, Mary has kept herself occupied with the work of grief. She has spent countless hours tending to Brittany's grave and to her roadside cross; she has copied CDs of photos for family and friends. She went through Brittany's belongings and gave some things to Goodwill and some to family. None of these tasks is yet complete, and she suspects she won't finish them for a long time. Often, the emotional weight they harbor catapults her back to the living room sofa, where she sits, sometimes for hours, uncharacteristically motionless and anchored.

She's not just being bowled over by her grief, although sometimes she is. Even in the days when she's physically doing nothing, she's working with it. She hates to be still, however. The night I visit her, ours is a conversation in motion. We start on the porch, where Mary smokes and drinks Dr. Pepper; and then, without warning, she is up and walking, to Brittany's room, where she has tried to contain her daughter's memorabilia out of respect and love for the other, living children. Hanging from the bed, several trendy belts still wait in neat rows: silver, brown, glittered cherry red. Then it's over to the computer room; then it's pacing the hallway; then walking to the garage out back. Then we return and do it all again.

In 2007, psychologist Yubal Neria surveyed a group of 9/11 families, a population known for making spontaneous memorials. Dr. Neria found that 43 percent were still experiencing "complicated grief," which he defined as "yearning for the deceased, preoccupation with the deceased that interrupts normal activities, trouble accepting the loss, detachment, bitterness, loneliness, feeling that life is empty, feeling that part of one's self died, and loss of security or safety."[15] Complicated grief, wrote Neria, is also commonly associated with loss of a child, especially a child of adult age.

If complicated grief lends itself to this constellation of agony, then it makes sense that an extraordinary number of the handmade memorials in the news seem to commemorate young adults in their teens and twenties. Of course, it could also be true that younger drivers are involved in more accidents. Or maybe it's just plain harder for someone who has lost a twenty-year-old son or daughter ever to feel better, and maybe such unending pain moves more people to want to publicly mark the spot of cataclysm.

Our nineteenth-century forebears didn't need a label like "complicated grief" to diagnose their mourning. The sheer quantity of death the average person experienced was Brobdingnagian compared to what the average American experiences today. That loss could be painful and sometimes deeply tragic, but it did not, I suspect, trigger the same sort of thunderbolt shock that unexpected death touches off today. In a sense, death in today's America is *always* unexpected. Even when it's not a literal surprise, it has a power, when first encountered, to deeply jar people who have come of age bathed in the deep unspoken conviction: This is not what is supposed to happen to us. To me. Like those strange dreams in which we find ourselves pushing open the door to a wing of our house we didn't know existed but now realize was there all along, death changes our conception of what life is.

For people living in the 1800s, the heavenly reunion that death brought *was* part of the natural course of events. So was grieving, in the socially mandated mourning process of the time. Yes, mourners removed themselves from everyday life, but the shadow world they inhabited was not a new wilderness. It was, rather, a place you inhabited, and then didn't, and then did again, at different times—a legitimate personal and social state complete with its own rules and regulations.

Today, there are no prescribed rules for mourning because it takes place outside the rest of American life, and awkward encounters like the one Mary Wilsey had at the florist's are a natural result of that. And maybe special classifications like "complicated grief" can have the effect of safely categorizing away people to whom horrific things happen, reassuring everyone else that catastrophe is not part of the regular course of human life. Not here, in twenty-first-century America.

Or maybe a designation like Dr. Neria's just helps map the territory of catastrophic loss, a land in dire need of a cartographer.

Had she lived in the 1800s, someone like Mary Wilsey could expect to be paid a measure of especial deference the rest of her life for this burden of grief she says she expects never to be fully rid of. As things are, here in early twenty-first-century America, her mourning contains in it an element that comes across as stubborn and combative. Frankly, I understand the flower shop clerk's nervousness. I myself am never quite comfortable. Mary is angry. I'm in no position to determine whether her emotional reaction to her own grief is justified; the presumption in that statement makes me feel queasy even to write it. But the effect her indignation has on me is certainly unsettling. Mary's personality, like that of her lost daughter, is combustible. She's quick to anger, and now she's angry because her daughter was killed. However, I wonder how much the flames of that anger are fanned by living among a people who are ill at ease with the concept of the full-time mourner. To what degree are they further fed by the notion that in America today, catastrophic death is just not supposed to happen?

In honoring our dead, we seek certain ends, no matter the method—and to some extent, no matter the era. Memorialization is holding on to someone after she's gone. It is wearing those heavy jet chains of sorrow and tending to a grave or a roadside cross or a timeworn memory every single day. Yet it is also the process by which we stop needing to do these things, the process by which we let go of the grief that sparked our need to do them. Thus it is a process, if it functions, that moves in opposing directions at the same time.

Everyone who purveys a certain kind of memorialization claims to do it right. To achieve a sense of closure—that ever-coveted state—

Ramsey Creek Preserve's Billy Campbell would say that the ideal way to do things is burial without embalming, with the full assistance of family. Certainly there's no grieving work more visceral than helping to lower your father's wicker casket into the ground yourself. In a major way, supporters of this cutting-edge yet ancient practice have the most in common with the group they are most popularly pitted against: traditional funeral directors.

"A funeral isn't a funeral unless there is a body present. That's what people need—to spend some time in the same room as their dead person. That's what gives them closure," wrote one commenter on the popular death-and-memorial blog *Final Embrace*.[16] He was responding to another funeral director's post bemoaning cremation's inexorable rise. From the wide world of Internet chatter, to *Frontline* specials, to funeral director Thomas Lynch's fabulous memoir *The Undertaking*, there's a clamor of late from the traditional funeral crowd. When we forgo the time-honored practices of embalming and viewing, they say, the real problem is not that we are harming their livelihoods, but that we are adding to our own alienation from humanity's natural processes.

Jessica Koth, with the National Funeral Directors Association, says, "I think that a lot of people think back ten, fifteen, twenty years ago, in the days of pancake makeup when people didn't always look really good. But the chemicals have changed, and the makeup that funeral directors use has changed dramatically. They're able to give people a much more natural appearance. So it's not the way you remember it." Funerals with embalmed bodies are no longer unpleasant, she says. Difficult, sure, but not unpleasant. Better by far, say many funeral directors, than the unembalmed bodies being carted out by the green burial camp: Despite the idealistic sentiments of green-burial advocates, not every person in grief can handle viewing an unembalmed dead body. After all, as large as our myth of the Beautiful Death looms in the popular imagination, people don't just fall asleep when they die. They suffer violent ends, be the culprit another person, a wasting illness, or an accident, and today's embalming techniques help erase the appearance of that violence so that, briefly, survivors are given what they want: the person made whole again, to say good-bye to.

However, there's something to Jessica Koth's statement that sticks in my head, despite her affirmation that funerals are still difficult. "It's not the way you remember it." Of course she's talking specifically about the movement away from the badly cosmetized bodies of yesteryear. But this part of her sentence, misquoted, sticks in my brain like an advertising jingle: "Death: Not the way you remember it." Inevitably, if "the way you remember" a funeral or memorial experience is horrible, then that horror stems at least in part from the grief that colors that memory absolutely, as well as from your deep and maybe even conflicted feelings about the person you've lost. And that discomfort is going to be there at any funeral, no matter how nice the body looks. There is no removal of the unpleasant, no removal of trauma, no death minus the Ghastly Specter itself.

My most vivid recollection of my grandmother's memorial service is the moment a cousin began wailing in grief when she beheld the plain wooden box of ashes up on the church's mantel. "That can't be her!" she screamed. "She can't be in that little box!" The memory of my cousin's outburst, which coincided with my own first view of the wooden box, churns my stomach the same way that the memory of viewing an embalmed body might stand out on the darker pages of someone else's life memories. The argument between the embalmers and the nonembalmers comes down, in a sense, to a question of reality, with each side claiming that the other is somehow fooling itself by avoiding the truth of death. And the converse: which side dwells on it too much.

Of course, Jessica Koth knows that no matter how, or whether, we choose to present the deceased, the fact of death cannot be excised from a memorial. There is no process completely free of distress or sadness or fear, no matter how much we decide to focus on the deceased's life rather than his or her death—whether by claiming that the embalmed body "looks so lifelike" or by substituting vibrant photographs in place of the dead person. But ignoring death doesn't banish it.

Poet Kathleen Sheeder Bonanno wrote an entire book of poems about the murder of her college-aged daughter by an ex-boyfriend. The last poem in the collection begins:

> You can try to strangle light:
> use your hands and think
> you've found the throat of it,
> but you haven't.
> You could use a rope or a garrote
> or a telephone cord,
> but the light, amorphous, implacable,
> will make a fool of you in the end.[17]

In a radio interview, Bonanno talked about the strange kernel of optimism inherent in grief itself. She says the process of mourning a daughter—the worst thing many of us can imagine—"is dark, but it's light."[18]

Death presents both sides of this knife: the shock of goneness, and the desire to show the world the spark of the life that has passed. Both of these slash through us at once, tearing and scarring. Someone dies. In the best of all worlds, what we do next depends on what feels honest regarding this horror of loss, the need to shepherd this soul or body to whatever comes next, and the need to honor the person we knew.

Cultural precepts change and dissolve into obscurity and oblivion, but certain constants remain. A mourner's world fills with unwitting, de facto mementos: a room in a house, a song, the unconscious gestures of surviving relatives. The trick is to choose the ideal surrogate object on which to displace our affection and tend lovingly, until the day we can stand not to. The stone, the tree, the canyon, the ocean. The small white wooden cross up on the hill, catching the final rays of sun before they leave this part of the earth.

AFTERWORD

In 2008, the Museum of Funeral Customs closed due to lack of revenue. Former curator Jon Austin says he was personally devastated by the shutdown of the place into which he'd poured so much research and personal dedication. However, today finds him continuing to educate the public about funeral history. He's one driving force behind the Abraham Lincoln Funeral Coalition, which will reenact the funeral procession and entombment of the sixteenth president on the 150th anniversary of his death in 2015. He also presents demonstrations simulating early embalming techniques at museums and public events. "I observe many 'lightbulb moments,'" he says, "when visitors connect what they know about their own funeral and burial experiences with what I tell them about the techniques and profession in the 1860s."

The tornado of 2008 set Oakland Cemetery back a year in its restoration efforts, producing some $1.5 million in losses. At the same time, the great storm was one of the best things to happen to Oakland. "It created an awareness," says director of volunteers and special events Mary Woodlan. "People said, 'Wow, that place really is fragile, isn't it? It's worth saving.'" With help from state and national emergency management agencies and waves of volunteers, the cemetery was repaired. These days, membership is up, and the future of the historic cemetery looks bright. Of course, it'll be years before its famous canopy looks anything like it once did; the storm felled more than one hundred trees, mostly oaks. But Mary points out that the uprooted trees were quite old and some of them dying. Storms are nature's way of housekeeping. "And we found that for several years after–I mean, *long* after we were like, 'Oh, my gosh. We are *over* that storm,'–the media would still be like, 'Well, what about that tornado?'" She throws up her hands and laughs.

Kevin Kuharic left his position as restoration director in 2010. He now lives in Colorado.

Sarah Peacock is still noted for her ultrarealistic work as a tattoo artist, but a motorcycle accident in 2009 that almost killed her husband sent her into an emotional tailspin. "It took me a long time to realize I was experiencing post-traumatic stress about it," she says. Later that year, she tattooed a realistic nipple onto a woman who had undergone reconstructive breast cancer surgery. That woman referred her to friends, who referred her to more friends, and now Sarah is the go-to tattoo artist for a leading reconstructive surgery clinic. Three or four days each week, she tattoos one of these clients–in the morning, before the regular tattoo business opens. "I ask them to cover my basic costs if they can afford to–but if they can't, I'll do it for free." She says that shepherding her husband through a traumatic medical experience gives her a deep rapport with these women. "Also, I live with my husband's scars on a daily basis, so their scars don't faze me." The whole thing has changed her outlook and her business, too, which now sponsors a number of charity events. "It's changed everything right around."

In 2012, Anne Gordon retired as a police chaplain in order to have more flexibility in her schedule for mission work. In the past five years, while traveling in Haiti, Kenya, China, and Mexico, she has instructed at a girls' orphanage, taught English to pastors and Bible students, and helped build a medical clinic. On mission trips, she's a firm believer in asking locals what their needs are and then doing the work to fill them, "rather than the old-fashioned western model of, 'This is what you're doing wrong, and this is what we think you should be doing.'"

In August 2011, a routine blood test diagnosed her husband, Bob, with Stage 3 colon cancer. He decided against any treatment and, after surprisingly little pain, died seven months later. Anne says that in those last months, his faith in God gave him a fabulous sense of humor about his condition. "Someone would wave to him as he was going on a walk, and he'd respond with a wave, 'Oh, yeah. Dead man walking!'"

She still works as an on-call chaplain for the funeral home. "Being a chaplain, I have the freedom to interact with people of different denominations, as well as nonbelievers. It's tremendous to have that freedom. To reach and out and touch someone of a different culture, to be able to reach out and say, 'Here, let me help you through this,' to me that's important. We've got to stop putting labels on people. That's why I enjoy doing it."

Oana Hogrefe quit her day job to become a full-time photographer of children and families in 2009. She still takes memorial photographs a couple of times a year, but not nearly as often as she used to, citing the long emotional recovery time. Now she gives away a photography package each year to a family facing serious medical challenges. She also shoots a calendar whose proceeds go to a children's charity.

Lesley Cullen has retired and lives the "beach bum" life, which includes a great deal of swimming and biking. She is happily remarried; she is now Lesley Mushalla. "And you think that when you remarry, you'll just move forward, but it's not exactly like that," she says. She still has hard days, especially in August, the month her late husband,

Bill, died. However, she also says that in the years since his death, she believes his soul has frequently visited the people he loved in life.

Seven months after seeing his wife's artificial coral reef ball placed on the ocean floor, Bob Allen died of brain cancer. His family returned to South Carolina the following fall to place a reef ball made with his ashes next to that of his wife.

After more than five decades of working at Wilkerson and Sons funeral home, Don Wilkerson retired in 2010.

Lenette Hall still runs the Urngarden and still says she'd like to quit. Last year, she had record-breaking sales every month.

Mary Wilsey continues to tend the roadside memorial for her daughter Brittany, but not as assiduously as she used to. An onerous struggle with depression makes visiting either the memorial or the little country cemetery that houses Brittany's grave "like taking ten steps back." Right now, she's doing a little bit better; she says her sons pretty much keep her going. "I hope that eventually I'll see her. But at least I don't wish that it was today."

ACKNOWLEDGMENTS

I appreciate the time, insights, and generosity of spirit of everyone whose names appear in these pages. Thanks to everyone at the University of North Carolina Wilmington who read early drafts and provided critical feedback, including Philip Gerard, Peter Trachtenberg, Clyde Edgerton, David Gessner, Wendy Brenner, Haven Kimmel, John Jeremiah Sullivan, Doug Diesenhaus, Corinne Manning, David Harris-Gershon, Visha Burkhart, Douglas Bourne, Adam Petry, Jason Matt, and so many others.

Financial support proved crucial in researching this work, and I am thankful to the Robert H. Byington Leadership Scholarship in Creative Writing and the Women's Resource Center at UNCW for providing it. I also owe an enormous debt to Liza Palmer for her tireless, enthusiastic research assistance. I cannot begin to express sufficient gratitude to my Wilmington comrades for their numerous insights, potluck suppers, and music breaks along the way, especially Erin Sroka, Ashley Hudson, Alison Harney, Janie Miller, Laurin Penland, Melissa Robon, and Geilda Barnett.

Thanks to critical readers and cheerleaders Eileen Drennen, Suzanne Van Atten, and Gina Webb, and to Sonya Huber, Jessica Handler, and Anna Schachner for helping me get there. I am abundantly grateful to Daren Wang for opening the door.

Thanks to the National Funeral Directors' Association; Kathleen Walczak and the Howard C. Raether Library; Mary Woodlan and David Moore with the Historic Oakland Foundation; the Green Burial Council; the Cremation Association of North America; the International Cemetery, Cremation and Funeral Association; Marilyn Johnson; the International Association of Obituarists; the Society of Professional Obituary Writers; and the Society of Allied and Independent Funeral Directors.

A heartfelt thanks to everyone at UGA Press, whose skill and commitment helped make this book what it is; and most of all to my best reader, Jon Black, without whose insights, bicycling breaks, and unswerving support and love I'd be nowhere, book or no book.

I gratefully acknowledge the following publications, where some of these chapters first appeared in altered form: *Oxford American*, *Atlanta Magazine*, and *New South*.

NOTES

CHAPTER 2.
GONE, BUT NOT FORGOTTEN

1. Heidler and Heidler, *Daily Life in the Early American Republic*, 135.

2. Jalland, *Death in the Victorian Family*, 2.

3. Ladd and Meyers, *Romanticism and Transcendentalism*, 16, 92.

4. Stowe, *Uncle Tom's Cabin*, original from Harvard University, digitized Sep 23, 2005, accessed March 24, 2009, http://books.google.com/books?id =sKOyVk5sG3IC&printsec=toc#PPA410,M1.

5. Faust, *This Republic of Suffering*, 30.

6. Young, *Our Deportment*, 338-39.

7. Coleman, *Courtaulds*, 84.

8. Young, *Our Deportment*, 339-40.

9. Coleman, *Courtaulds*, 84.

10. Maureen DeLorme, "Artes Moriendi: Death Art from the Middle Ages to the Victorian Age," *Mortuary Management*, May 1998, 13-14.

11. Ames, *Death in the Dining Room*, 147-49.

12. Quoted in DeLorme, "Artes Moriendi," 20.

13. "Hair Work," *Godey's Lady Book*, 1851, accessed March 24, 2009, http://digitalgallery.nypl.org/nypldigital/id?831705.

14. Eichler, *Book of Etiquette*, 84, 85.

15. Lillian C. Bragg, "Hair and Mourning Jewelry," *Hobbies: The Magazine for Collectors*, October 1945, 12.

16. Stéphane Audoin-Rouzeau and Annette Becker, *Understanding the Great War* (New York: Hill and Wang, 2003), 224, 225.

17. Eichler, *Book of Etiquette*, 89, 91, 96.

CHAPTER 3.
THE CEMETERY'S CEMETERY

1. Sloane, *The Last Great Necessity*, 28.

2. Ibid., 86.

3. *Rochester Daily Union and Advertiser*, June 6, 1861, quoted in Sloane, *The Last Great Necessity*, 86.

4. Kaemmerlen, *The Historic Oakland Cemetery of Atlanta*, 57.

5. Conway, *The Reconstruction of Georgia*, 24, 25.

DISMAL TRADE.
KAY POWELL, OBITUARY WRITER

1. Stacy Lynch, Mary Nesbitt, and Steven Duke, "Inside Satisfaction: What It Means, How to Increase It," *Readership Institute*, 2002, accessed August 6, 2012, http://www.readership.org/content/editorial/data/elements_of_satisfaction.pdf.

CHAPTER 4.
THE LAST GREAT OBIT WRITERS' CONFERENCE

1. Folke Dahl, *A Bibliography of English Corantos and Periodical Newsbooks 1620–1642*, 18, quoted in Starck, *Life after Death*, 3–4.

2. Habenstein and Lamers, *The History of American Funeral Directing*, 207.

3. Obituary of John Chestnutt, *National Intelligencer*, May 9, 1818, quoted in Janice Hume, *Obituaries in American Culture*, 32.

4. Ibid., 82–83.

5. Obituary of Mark Walton, *New Orleans Picayune*, December 4, 1870, quoted in ibid., 83.

6. Ibid., 46, 88.

7. Ibid., 31–32, 115.

8. Margalit Fox, "Hugh Massingberd, 60, Laureate for the Departed, Dies," *New York Times*, December 30, 2007, accessed August 15, 2008, http://www.nytimes.com/2007/12/30/nyregion/30massingberd.html.

9. Eagleman, *Sum*, 23.

10. Sheeler, "Your Life Must Be So Dull," *Obit*, 59.

11. Claire Martin, "Preemie's Hard-Fought Battle Ends in Arms of Father," *Denver Post*, A-30, May 18, 2003.

12. Alex Beam, "Grave Schism on the Death Beat," *Boston Globe*, June 2, 2008, accessed August 15, 2008, http://www.boston.com/lifestyle/articles/2008/06/03/grave_schism_on_the_death_beat/.

CHAPTER 6.

THE HOUSE WHERE DEATH LIVES

1. W. Osler and T. McCrae, *The Principles and Practice of Medicine* (New York: D. Appleton and Company, 1920), 102.

2. "Booming Michigan: W. S. Anderson Has Something to Say About the Next Annual Meeting," *The Casket*, February 1891.

3. "Home-Made Coffins: They Are Still Plentiful in Kentucky–Suggestion Concerning Embalming Schools," *The Casket*, March 1, 1898.

4. R. B. Lanum, "Grave Torpedo," *The Casket*, July 1, 1880.

5. Joel E. Crandall, "Demisurgery: The New Art in Undertaking," *The Sunnyside*, April 15, 1912.

6. *Embalmers' Monthly*, February 1895.

7. Faust, *This Republic of Suffering*, 89–98.

8. "Model Establishments. Elegant Quarters of the Frank C. Reavy Estate at Cohoes–A Model of Completeness and Up-to-Dateness," *The Casket*, December 1, 1905.

9. "A Notable Illinois Establishment: The John T. Downs 'Funeral Home' at Aurora," *Embalmers' Monthly*, August 1915.

10. Cotton Mather, "Perswasions from the Terror of the Lord. A Sermon Concerning, the Day of Judgment; Preached on a Solemn Occasion," 1711.

11. Diary of Samuel Sewall, 2: 658.

12. Jonathan Edwards, unpublished sermon in Edwards's manuscripts in Yale University Library, quoted in Stannard, *The Puritan Way of Death*, 65.

13. William Thompson, *The Duty of a People Respecting their Deceased Ministers* (Boston, 1742), 12-13, quoted in ibid., 150.

14. Ibid., 189-191.

15. Thomas Lynch, "A Serious Undertaking," *Washington Post*, August 3, 2001; http://www.thomaslynch.com/1/234/washington_post.asp?artID=16485 (accessed March 16, 2013).

DISMAL TRADE.

ANNE GORDON, FUNERAL CHAPLAIN

1. Joanne Silberner, "Britain Weighs Social Cost of 'Wonder' Drugs," *NPR*, July 23, 2008, accessed January 27, 2009, http://www.npr.org/templates/story/story.php?storyId=91996282.

2. Farrell, *Inventing the American Way of Death*, 60.

CHAPTER 8.

DEATH BY THE ROADSIDE

1. California Department of Transportation, "Signs and Workzones Branch: Victims Memorial Sign Program," January 4, 2007, accessed November 14, 2008, http://www.dot.ca.gov/hq/traffops/signtech/signdel/victims.htm.

2. *The People of the State of Colorado v. Rodney Lyle Scott*, 00-<nsc>m</nsc>-2096, Adams County court, 2001, quoted in "Colorado Court Rules Roadside Cross 'Litter,' Not 'Venerated Object,'" *Freethought Today*, Freedom from Religion Foundation, June/July 2001, accessed November 14, 2008, http://www.ffrf.org/fttoday/2001/junejuly01/colorado.html.

3. Bill McGraw, "To Honor Cyclist, Tribute Gone," *Detroit Free Press*, October 3, 2008, accessed November 14, 2008, http://www.freep.com/article/20081003/COL27/810030362.

4. "Committee Minutes," Alaska State Legislature, March 27, 2003, accessed November 14, 2008, http://www.legis.state.ak.us/basis/get_single_minute.asp?session=23&house=H&comm=STA&date=20030327&time=0801.

5. Ginny MacDonald, "Birmingham-Area Transportation Officials Order Roadside Memorials Removed from Interstates," *Birmingham News*, May 6, 2008, accessed November 15, 2008, http://www.al.com/news/birminghamnews/index.ssf?/base/news/1210061777198420.xml.

6. Roadside Memorials sales page, accessed November 15, 2008, http://roadsidememorials.com/order.html.

7. Anonymous online comment, July 11, 2008, responding to Patrick Gannon, "Officials Ask Family to Take Down Roadside Memorial," *Wilmington Star*, July 11, 2008, accessed November 6, 2008, http://www.starnewsonline.com/article/20080711/ARTICLE/807110301.

8. Jim Dooley, "Driver who killed 2 teens avoids jail," *Honolulu Star Advertiser*, January 22, 2009, accessed November 19, 2012, http://the.honoluluadvertiser.com/article/2009/Jan/22/ln/hawaii901220343.html.

9. Anonymous online comment, July 11, 2008, commenting on Patrick Gannon, "Officials Ask Family," *Wilmington Star.*

10. Anonymous online comment, October 21, 2008, responding to Kerry Lester, "A Memory, and a Message," *Daily Herald*, October 11, 2008, accessed November 6, 2008, http://www.dailyherald.com/story/?id=24417 7#storycomments.

11. Habenstein and Lamers, *The History of American Funeral Directing*, 204.

12. Earle, *Customs and Fashions*, 376.

13. Ludwig, *Graven Images*, 60.

14. Habenstein and Lamers, *The History of American Funeral Directing*, 212.

15. Yuval Neria and others, "Prevalence and Psychological Correlates of Complicated Grief Among Bereaved Adults 2.5–3.5 Years After September 11th Attacks," *Journal of Traumatic Stress* 20, no. 3 (June 2007): 251-262.

16. Tim Totten, "Just Another Celebrity Cremation," *Final Embrace: Funeral Industry News, Marketing Tips, and Management Advice*, January 12, 2009, accessed January 21, 2009. http://finalembrace.com/2009/01/12/just-another-celebrity-cremation/#comment-21181.

17. Bonanno, "Poem About Light," *Slamming Open the Door.*

18. "On the Page, Poet Mourns Daughter's Murder," Transcript, *NPR*, July 29, 2009, accessed September 4, 2009, http://www.npr.org/templates/transcript/transcript.php?storyId=111218053.

BIBLIOGRAPHY

Ames, Kenneth. *Death in the Dining Room and Other Tales of Victorian Culture*. Philadelphia: Temple University Press, 1992.

Ball, John C., and Jill Jonnes. *Fame at Last: Who Was Who According to the New York Times Obituaries*. Kansas City: Andrews McMeel, 2000.

Bonanno, Kathleen Sheeler. *Slamming Open the Door*. Farmington, Maine: Alice James Books, 2009.

Coffin, Margaret M. *Death in Early America*. New York: Elsevier/Nelson Books, 1976.

Coleman, Donald Cuthbert. *Courtaulds: An Economic and Social History*. Vol. 2. London: Oxford University Press, 1969.

Conway, Alan. *The Reconstruction of Georgia*. Minneapolis: University of Minnesota Press, 1966.

Eagleman, Dave. *Sum: Forty Tales from the Afterlives*. New York: Pantheon Books, 2009.

Earle, Alice Morse. *Customs and Fashions in Old New England*. New York: Charles Scribner's Sons, 1894.

Eichler, Lillian. *Book of Etiquette*. Vol. 1. New York: Nelson Doubleday, 1923.

Farrell, James J. *Inventing the American Way of Death*. Philadelphia: Temple University Press, 1980.

Faust, Drew Gilpin. *This Republic of Suffering: Death and the American Civil War*. New York: Random House, 2008.

Gittings, Peter C., and Clare Gittings, eds. *Death in England: An Illustrated History*. New Brunswick, N.J.: Rutgers University Press, 2000.

Habenstein, Robert W., and William M. Lamers. *The History of American Funeral Directing*. Rev. ed. Milwaukee: Bulfin, 1962.

Heidler, David S., and Jeanne T. Heidler. *Daily Life in the Early American Republic, 1790–1820: Creating a New Nation*. Westport, Conn.: Greenwood Press, 2004.

Houghton, Walter R. *American Etiquette and Rules of Politeness*. Chicago: Rand McNally, 1882.

Hume, Janice. *Obituaries in American Culture*. Jackson: University Press of Mississippi, 2000.

Jalland, Pat. *Death in the Victorian Family*. Oxford: Oxford University Press, 1996.

Kaemmerlen, Cathy J. *The Historic Oakland Cemetery of Atlanta: Speaking Stones*. Charleston, S.C.: History Press, 2007.

Ladd, Andrew, and Karen Meyers. *Romanticism and Transcendentalism: 1800–1860*. Storrs, Conn.: Chelsea House, 2006, 2010.

Laderman, Gary. *Rest in Peace: A Cultural History of Death and the Funeral Home in Twentieth-Century America*. New York: Oxford University Press, 2003.

Ludwig, Allan I. *Graven Images: New England Stonecarving and Its Symbols, 1650–1815*. Hanover, N.H.: University of New England Press, 1999.

Sheeler, Jim. *Obit: Inspiring Stories of Ordinary People Who Led Extraordinary Lives*. Boulder: Pruett, 2007.

Sloane, David Charles. *The Last Great Necessity: Cemeteries in American History*. Baltimore: Johns Hopkins University Press, 1991.

Starck, Nigel. *Life after Death: The Art of the Obituary*. Melbourne: Melbourne University Press, 2006.

Stannard, David E. *The Puritan Way of Death: A Study in Religion, Culture, and Social Change*. New York: Oxford University Press, 1977.

Stowe, Harriet Beecher. *Uncle Tom's Cabin, or, Life among the Lowly*. Philadelphia: H. Altemus, 1900.

Young, John H. *Our Deportment*. Detroit: F. B. Dickerson, 1881.